WITHDRAWN

Economic Sanctions

Other Books in the Global Viewpoints Series

GLOBALVIEWPOINTS

Economic Sanctions

Kristina Lyn Heitkamp, Book Editor

GREENHAVEN
PUBLISHING

Published in 2019 by Greenhaven Publishing, LLC
353 3rd Avenue, Suite 255, New York, NY 10010

Articles in Greenhaven Publishing anthologies are often edited for length to meet page
requirements. In addition, original titles of these works are changed to clearly present
the main thesis and to explicitly indicate the author's opinion. Every effort is made to
ensure that Greenhaven Publishing accurately reflects the original intent of the authors.
Every effort has been made to trace the owners of the copyrighted material.

Cover image: KENA BETANCUR/AFP/Getty Images

Library of Congress Cataloging-in-Publication Data

Names: Heitkamp, Kristina Lyn, editor.
Title: Economic sanctions / Kristina Lyn Heitkamp, book editor.
Description: First edition. | New York : Greenhaven Publishing, 2019. |
  Series: Global viewpoints | Includes bibliographical references and index. | Audience:
  Grades 9-12.
Identifiers: LCCN 2018005371| ISBN 9781534503434 (library bound) | ISBN
  9781534503441 (pbk.)
Subjects: LCSH: Economic sanctions--Juvenile literature.
Classification: LCC HF1413.5 .E2656 2019 | DDC 327.1/17--dc23
LC record available at https://lccn.loc.gov/2018005371

Manufactured in the United States of America

Website: http://greenhavenpublishing.com

Contents

Chapter 2: Efficacy of Economic Sanctions

Chapter 3: Economic Sanctions and Terrorism

Chapter 4: The Future of Economic Sanctions

Foreword

| "*The problems of all of humanity can only be solved by all of humanity.*"
| —*Swiss author Friedrich Dürrenmatt*

Global interdependence has become an undeniable reality. Mass media and technology have increased worldwide access to information and created a society of global citizens. Understanding and navigating this global community is a challenge, requiring a high degree of information literacy and a new level of learning sophistication.

Building on the success of its flagship series, Opposing Viewpoints, Greenhaven Publishing has created the Global Viewpoints series to examine a broad range of current, often controversial topics of worldwide importance from a variety of international perspectives. Providing students and other readers with the information they need to explore global connections and think critically about worldwide implications, each Global Viewpoints volume offers a panoramic view of a topic of widespread significance.

Drugs, famine, immigration—a broad, international treatment is essential to do justice to social, environmental, health, and political issues such as these. Junior high, high school, and early college students, as well as general readers, can all use Global Viewpoints anthologies to discern the complexities relating to each issue. Readers will be able to examine unique national perspectives while, at the same time, appreciating the interconnectedness that global priorities bring to all nations and cultures.

Material in each volume is selected from a diverse range of sources, including journals, magazines, newspapers, nonfiction books, speeches, government documents, pamphlets, organization newsletters, and position papers. Global Viewpoints is truly global, with material drawn primarily from international sources available in English and secondarily from US sources with extensive international coverage.

Features of each volume in the Global Viewpoints series include:

- An **annotated table of contents** that provides a brief summary of each essay in the volume, including the name of the country or area covered in the essay.

- An **introduction** specific to the volume topic.

- A **world map** to help readers locate the countries or areas covered in the essays.

- For each viewpoint, an **introduction** that contains notes about the author and source of the viewpoint explains why material from the specific country is being presented, summarizes the main points of the viewpoint, and offers three **guided reading questions** to aid in understanding and comprehension.

- **For further discussion questions** that promote critical thinking by asking the reader to compare and contrast aspects of the viewpoints or draw conclusions about perspectives and arguments.

- A worldwide list of **organizations to contact** for readers seeking additional information.

- A **periodical bibliography** for each chapter and a **bibliography of books** on the volume topic to aid in further research.

- A comprehensive **subject index** to offer access to people, places, events, and subjects cited in the text.

Global Viewpoints is designed for a broad spectrum of readers who want to learn more about current events, history, political science, government, international relations, economics, environmental science, world cultures, and sociology—students doing research for class assignments or debates, teachers and faculty seeking to supplement course materials, and others wanting to understand current issues better. By presenting how people in various countries perceive the root causes, current consequences, and proposed solutions to worldwide challenges, Global Viewpoints volumes offer readers opportunities to enhance their global awareness and their knowledge of cultures worldwide.

Introduction

"Sanctions are a sign of irritation; they are not the instrument of serious policies."
— Sergei Lavrov, the Russian Foreign
Minister responding to European
Union sanctions imposed on Moscow

With the international exchange of goods and services, the modern world has advanced into a complex and connected global economy. Fossil fuels, clothing, cars, and even gadgets are all evidence of the world economy. Because the system is so interdependent, countries can use this relationship to influence. Economic sanctions are a foreign policy tool used by a country or international organization, such as the United Nations, to punish or persuade another country into action. The sanction can restrict trade, halt investments or disrupt commercial activity. A carrot and stick approach, the economic pressure aims to alter a government's political course, reform ethical standards, and compel a change in behavior. Sanctions can also be applied as a precursor or placeholder until more punitive action is taken, such as war.

The concept of sanctions has been around for at least a few thousand years, since the ancient Greeks. In 432 BCE Athens enforced the Megarian Decree on its neighbor city of Megara. Similar to a modern day trade embargo, the merchants of Megara were denied access to Athens's market, as well as the ports in its empire. Some scholars believe the sanctions were an act of revenge for previous wrongdoings, while others deem it was political move to maintain power. Regardless of motive, the sanctions inadvertently ignited the Peloponnesian War.

Economic sanctions can blanket an entire country, such as in the case of the international sanctions against North Korea as punishment for cyberattacks, money laundering, human rights violations, and development of nuclear weapons. Or sanctions can target businesses, groups, or individual citizens, such as the international sanctions against South Africa and its apartheid regime during the 1970s and 1980s. Civil society groups around the world, including local governments, universities, and labor unions, all cut financial ties to the apartheid government. The massive divestment withdrew $20 billion from companies doing business in the country.

Sanctions also have been used to counter terrorism, helping to thwart states from funding terrorist activity. Yet some policy makers argue that economic sanctions do little against the hosts of transnational terrorists, or may target states with no tie to terrorism.

Whether economic sanctions are a response to geopolitical changes or employed to counter terrorism, the efficacy of the foreign policy tool is debated. Critics say sanctions are often not put together well and are rarely successful. Sanctions have a track record of unintended consequences, such as harming innocent civilians or encouraging black market trade. Sometimes the economic punishment is not dramatic enough to motivate change. Fear of retaliation is also a concern. The *New York Times* reported on North Korea's July 2017 response to imposed sanctions.

> In a staccato of outraged reactions on Monday to the sanctions imposed over the weekend, North Korea threatened retaliation against the United States "thousands of times" over, vowed to never give up its nuclear arsenal and called the penalties a panicky response by an American bully.
>
> But it is unclear at best, experts on sanctions say, whether the measures will hinder North Korea's nuclear militarization or even crimp its economy.[1]

However, proponents tout that sanctions are an effective and essential foreign policy tool. Successful sanctions have multilateral support from several states and are universally applied. Following through with imposed conditions and securing attainable goals help sanctions perform how they are intended. Some scholars say that economic sanctions may not be a silver bullet answer, but when goals are flexible and supplemented with incentives, they can be instrumental in achieving the desired outcome.

Regardless of degrees of efficacy or failure, economic sanctions remain a foreign policy tool. Sanctions continue to lead news headlines, and center the debate of political pundits and economists. Business and economic scholars analyze the ethics of sanctions, and how they impact global relationships. *Global Viewpoints: Economic Sanctions* presents diverse viewpoints from around the world that consider the many facets of the controversial tool, and evaluate their future.

Endnotes
1. Jane Perlez and Rick Gladstone, "North Korea Rails Against New Sanctions. Whether They Will Work Is Unclear," *New York Times*, Aug 7, 2017.

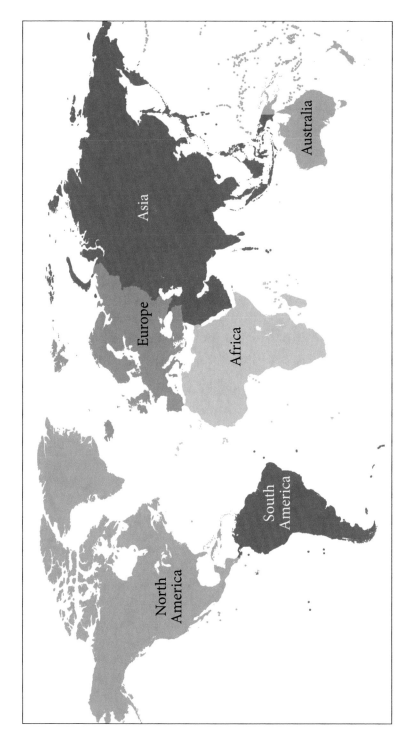

GLOBALVIEWPOINTS

CHAPTER 1

Economic Sanctions Around the World

Sanction Success Depends on Best Practices

Jonathan Masters

In the following viewpoint, Jonathan Masters offers a detailed primer on different types of economic sanctions and how they are used. He explains the sanction process of both the United States and European Union. Masters highlights how secondary sanctions may be considered a violation of sovereignty and international law. However, he argues that targeted sanctions can be successful if employed with certain considerations. Masters is a deputy editor at the Council on Foreign Relations, and writes about national security and civil liberties issues. His work has been published with PBS NewsHour, The Atlantic, Newsweek, NBC, CNN, and Bloomberg.

As you read, consider the following questions:

1. How is the EU sanction process different from the US sanction process?
2. How did the USA Patriot Act change the power of the Treasury Department in the sanction process?
3. According to the author, what should be considered when evaluating the effectiveness of sanctions?

"What Are Economic Sanctions?" by Jonathan Masters, Council on Foreign Relations, August 7, 2017. Reprinted by permission.

G overnments and multinational bodies impose economic sanctions to try to alter the strategic decisions of state and nonstate actors that threaten their interests or violate international norms of behavior. Critics say sanctions are often poorly conceived and rarely successful in changing a target's conduct, while supporters contend they have become more effective in recent years and remain an essential foreign policy tool. Sanctions have become the defining feature of the Western response to several geopolitical challenges, including North Korea's nuclear program and Russia's intervention in Ukraine.

What Are Economic Sanctions?

Economic sanctions are defined as the withdrawal of customary trade and financial relations for foreign and security policy purposes. They may be comprehensive, prohibiting commercial activity with regard to an entire country, like the long-standing US embargo of Cuba, or they may be targeted, blocking transactions of and with particular businesses, groups, or individuals.

Since 9/11, there has been a pronounced shift toward targeted or so-called "smart" sanctions, which aim to minimize the suffering of innocent civilians. Sanctions take a variety of forms, including travel bans, asset freezes, arms embargoes, capital restraints, foreign aid reductions, and trade restrictions. (General export controls, which are not punitive, are often excluded from sanctions discussions.)

When Are Sanctions Used?

National governments and international bodies like the United Nations and European Union have imposed economic sanctions to coerce, deter, punish, or shame entities that endanger their interests or violate international norms of behavior. They have been used to advance a range of foreign policy goals, including counterterrorism, counternarcotics, nonproliferation, democracy and human rights promotion, conflict resolution, and cybersecurity.

Sanctions, while a form of intervention, are generally viewed as a lower-cost, lower-risk, middle course of action between diplomacy and war. Policymakers may consider sanctions a response to foreign crises in which the national interest is less than vital or where military action is not feasible. Leaders can on occasion issue sanctions while they evaluate more punitive action. For example, the UN Security Council imposed comprehensive sanctions against Iraq just four days after Saddam Hussein's invasion of Kuwait in August 1990. The Council did not authorize the use of military force until months later.

What Is the Sanctions Process at the UN?

As the UN's principal crisis-management body, the Security Council may respond to global threats by cutting economic ties with state and nonstate groups. Sanctions resolutions must pass the fifteen-member Council by a majority vote and without a veto from any of the five permanent members: the United States, China, France, Russia, and the United Kingdom. The most common types of UN sanctions, which are binding on all member states, are asset freezes, travel bans, and arms embargoes.

UN sanctions regimes are typically managed by a special committee and a monitoring group. The global police agency Interpol assists some sanctions committees, particularly those concerning al-Qaeda and the Taliban, but the UN has no independent means of enforcement and relies on member states, many of which have limited resources and little political incentive. Anecdotal evidence suggests that enforcement is often weak.

Prior to 1990, the Council imposed sanctions against just two states: Southern Rhodesia (1966) and South Africa (1977). However, since the end of the Cold War, the body has used sanctions more than twenty times, most often targeting parties to an intrastate conflict, as in Somalia, Liberia, and Yugoslavia in the 1990s. But despite this cooperation, sanctions are often divisive, reflecting the competing interests of world powers. For instance, since 2011, Russia and China have vetoed several Security Council resolutions concerning the conflict in Syria, some of which could have led to sanctions against President Bashar al-Assad's regime.

What Is the Sanctions Process in the EU?

The European Union imposes sanctions (known more commonly in the twenty-eight-member bloc as restrictive measures) as part of its Common Foreign and Security Policy. Because the EU lacks a joint military force, many European leaders consider sanctions the bloc's most powerful foreign policy tool. Sanctions policies must receive unanimous consent from member states in the Council of the European Union, the body that represents EU leaders.

Since its inception in 1992, the EU has levied sanctions more than thirty times (in addition to those mandated by the UN). Analysts say the comprehensive sanctions imposed on Iran in 2012 marked a turning point for the bloc, which had previously sought to limit sanctions to specific individuals or companies. Individual states may impose harsher sanctions independently within their national jurisdiction.

What Is the Sanctions Process in the United States?

The United States uses economic and financial sanctions more than any other country. Sanctions policy may originate in either the executive or legislative branches. Presidents typically launch the process by issuing an executive order (EO) that declares a national emergency in response to an "unusual and extraordinary" foreign threat, such as "the proliferation of nuclear, biological, and chemical weapons" (EO 12938) or "the actions and policies of the Government of the Russian Federation with respect to Ukraine" (EO 13661). This affords the president special powers (pursuant to the International Emergency Economic Powers Act) to regulate commerce with regard to that threat for a period of one year, unless extended by him/her or terminated by a joint resolution of Congress. (Executive orders may also modify sanctions.)

Notably, most of the more than fifty states of emergency declared since Congress placed limits on their duration in 1976 remain in effect today, including the first, ordered by President Jimmy Carter in 1979 with respect to Iran.

Congress, for its part, may pass legislation imposing new sanctions or modifying existing ones, which it has done in many cases. In instances where there are multiple legal authorities, as with Cuba and Iran, congressional and executive action may be required to alter or lift the restrictions. In July 2017, Congress passed and President Donald Trump reluctantly signed a bill adding to the list of sanctions on Russia, Iran, and North Korea. The bill is noteworthy in that it requires the president to justify to the legislature any termination of the sanctions.

For the most part, the twenty-six existing US sanctions programs are administered by the Treasury Department's Office of Foreign Assets Control (OFAC), while other departments, including State, Commerce, Homeland Security, and Justice, may also play an integral role. For instance, the secretary of state can designate a group a Foreign Terrorist Organization, or label a country a State Sponsor of Terrorism, both of which have sanctions implications. (Travel bans are handled by the State Department as well.) State and local authorities, particularly in New York, may also contribute to enforcement efforts.

In 2017, the United States had comprehensive sanctions regimes on Cuba, Iran, Sudan, and Syria, as well as more than a dozen other programs targeting individuals and entities pertaining to certain political crises or suspected of certain types of criminal behavior, such as narcotics trafficking. OFAC routinely adds (or deletes) entries on its blacklist of more than six thousand individuals, businesses, and groups (known as Specially Designated Nationals). The assets of those listed are blocked, and US persons, including US businesses and their foreign branches, are forbidden from transacting with them.

How Did the 9/11 Attacks Change Sanctions Policy?

In concert with its allies, the US government launched an all-out effort to disrupt the financial infrastructure supporting terrorists and international criminals. This campaign focused on the gateways

US Economic Sanctions Policy and Implementation

The Office of Economic Sanctions Policy and Implementation (EB/TFS/SPI) is responsible for developing and implementing foreign policy-related sanctions adopted to counter threats to national security posed by particular activities and countries. SPI builds international support for implementation of economic sanctions, provides foreign policy guidance to the Department of Treasury and Commerce on sanctions implementation, and works with Congress to draft legislation that advances U.S. foreign policy goals in these areas. SPI maintains and enforces sanctions to maximize their economic impact on our targets and minimize the damage to U.S. economic interests. We also work to remove economic sanctions when appropriate to reward and incentivize improved behavior or demonstrate U.S. support for newly established democratic governments. In addition, SPI conducts outreach on sanctions issues to a wide range of interested parties including NGOs, companies, diaspora groups, and others.

"Economic Sanctions Policy and Implementation," U.S. Department of State.

of the global financial system—international banks—and relied on a handful of new authorities granted to US agents in the days after the attacks.

On September 23, President George W. Bush signed EO 13224 that provided Treasury Department officials with far-reaching authority to freeze the assets and financial transactions of individuals and other entities suspected of supporting terrorism. Weeks later, Bush gave the Treasury broad powers (under Section 311 of the USA Patriot Act) to designate foreign jurisdictions and financial institutions as "primary money laundering concerns." (Notably, Treasury needs only a reasonable suspicion—not necessarily any evidence—to target entities under these laws.)

Experts say that these measures fundamentally reshaped the financial regulatory environment, greatly raising the risks for banks and other institutions engaged in suspicious activity, even unwittingly. The centrality of New York and the dollar to the global financial system mean these US policies are felt globally.

Penalties for sanctions violations can be huge in terms of fines, loss of business, and reputational damage. Federal and state authorities have been particularly rigorous in prosecuting banks in recent years, settling at least fifteen cases with fines over $100 million since 2009. In a record settlement, France's largest lender, BNP Paribas, pleaded guilty in 2014 to processing billions of dollars for blacklisted Cuban, Iranian, and Sudanese entities. The bank was fined nearly $9 billion—by far the largest such penalty in history—and lost the right to convert foreign currency into dollars for certain types of transactions for one year.

Similarly, those tainted by a US money-laundering designation may suffer crippling losses. In September 2005, Treasury officials labeled Banco Delta Asia a primary money laundering concern, alleging that the Macau-based bank was a "willing pawn for the North Korean government." Within a week, customers withdrew $133 million, or 34 percent of BDA's deposits. The financial shock rippled across the globe, inducing other international banks to sever ties with Pyongyang.

"This new approach worked by focusing squarely on the behavior of financial institutions rather than on the classic sanctions framework of the past," wrote Juan Zarate, a top Bush administration official involved in counterterrorism efforts, in his book *Treasury's War* (2013). "In this new approach, the policy decisions of government are not nearly as persuasive as the risk-based compliance calculus of financial institutions."

What Are Extraterritorial Sanctions?

Traditionally, sanctions prohibit only a home country's or region's corporations and citizens from doing business with a blacklisted entity. (Unlike UN sanctions, which are global by nature.) However, extraterritorial sanctions (sometimes called secondary sanctions or a secondary boycott) are designed to restrict the economic activity of governments, businesses, and nationals of third countries. As a result, many governments consider these sanctions a violation of their sovereignty and international law.

In recent years, the reach of US sanctions continued to draw the ire of some close allies. France's leadership criticized the US prosecution of BNP Paribas as "unfair" and indicated there would be "negative consequences" on bilateral as well as US-EU relations. "The extraterritoriality of American standards, linked to the use of the dollar, should drive Europe to mobilize itself to advance the use of the euro as a currency for international trade," said French Finance Minister Michel Sapin.

Do Sanctions Work?

Many scholars and practitioners say that sanctions, particularly targeted sanctions, can be at least partly successful and should remain in the tool kits of foreign policymakers. Evaluations of sanctions should consider the following:

- The dynamics of each historical case vary immensely. Sanctions effective in one setting may fail in another, depending on countless factors. Sanctions programs with relatively limited objectives are generally more likely to succeed than those with major political ambitions. Furthermore, sanctions may achieve their desired economic effect, but they may fail to change behavior. UN sanctions on Afghanistan in 2000 and 2001 exacted a heavy toll but failed to move the Taliban regime to surrender Osama bin Laden.

- Sanctions often evolve over time. A classic illustration of this is the US regime on Iran. Except for a brief period in the 1980s, Washington has had sanctions on Tehran since US hostages were taken in 1979. However, the scope of these measures and the logic behind them have changed dramatically.

- Only correlations, not causal relationships, can be determined. For example, many believe UN sanctions imposed on Liberia in 2003 helped bring about the collapse of the Charles Taylor regime, but any number of domestic and international factors could have played more decisive roles.

- The comparative utility of sanctions is what matters and not simply whether they achieve their objective. US-EU sanctions against Russia may not stem the crisis in Ukraine, but other courses of action, including inaction, may have fared worse (and cost more). In some cases, sanctions may simply be intended as an expression of opprobrium.

Meanwhile, experts cite several best practices in developing sanctions policy:

- Develop a well-rounded approach. An effective strategy often links punitive measures, like sanctions and the threat of military action, with positive inducements, like financial aid. Some point to the Libya strategy adopted by the United States and its allies in the late 1990s and early 2000s.

- Set attainable goals. Sanctions aimed at regime change or that offer the target little recourse except what it believes would be political suicide are likely to fail. Many cite the US embargo on the Castro regime as a cautionary tale.

- Build multilateral support. The more governments that sign on to (and enforce) sanctions the better, especially in cases where the target is economically diversified. Sanctions against South Africa's apartheid regime in the 1980s, Saddam Hussein's Iraq in the 1990s, or on Iran and Russia today would not be nearly as powerful without multilateral support.

- Be credible and flexible. The target must believe that sanctions will be increased or reduced based on its behavior. In 2012, the Obama administration responded to major political reforms in Myanmar by easing some financial and investment restrictions. It ended the sanctions program in 2016.

The Positive Economic Implications of Lifting Sanctions on Iran

Shanta Devarajan and Lili Mottaghi

In the following excerpted viewpoint, Shanta Devarajan and Lili Mottaghi trace the economic effects of lifting sanctions on Iran. Their report follows the economic outcomes of international sanctions on Iran from 1979 to 2015. Removing sanctions not only hits the Iranian economy and its trading partners, but also affects the world oil market. Devarajan is the Senior Director for Development Economics (DEC) at the World Bank. Mottaghi is a Senior Economist in the Chief Economist Office for the World Bank's Middle East and North Africa Region. She works on economic growth, international trade and policy reform issues in developing and transition economies.

As you read, consider the following questions:

1. How would lifting sanctions on Iran affect the world oil price?
2. Which Iranian economic sectors would benefit from removal of sanctions?
3. According to the report, which is the most significant aspect of sanctions relief, and why?

Shanta Devarajan, Lili Mottaghi. 2015 "Economic Implications of Lifting Sanctions on Iran" Middle East and North Africa Quarterly Economic Brief, (July), World Bank, Washington, DC. http://documents.worldbank.org/curated/en/575391468187800406/pdf/98389-REVISION-BRI-PUBLIC-Box393170B-QEB-issue-5-FINAL-7-27-15.pdf. Licensed under CC BY 3.0 IGO.

Normally a quiet month before the August break, July has been unusually active for the global economy this year. First, there was Greece's debt crisis, a referendum on the terms of a bailout, and ensuing negotiations over debt relief. Next, China's stock market plunged by about 30 percent from its mid-June peak, stoking fears that the growth slowdown may be sharper than expected. Finally, Iran and the Permanent Members of the UN Security Council and Germany (P5+1) reached a deal on July 14, 2015 that limits Iranian nuclear activity in return for lifting all international sanctions that were placed on Iran (Box 1). This issue of the MENA Quarterly Economic Brief (QEB) traces the economic effects of the latter development—removing sanctions on Iran—on the world oil market, on Iran's trading partners, and on the Iranian economy.

The most significant change will be Iran's return to the oil market. The World Bank estimates that the eventual addition of one million barrels a day (mb/d) from Iran, assuming no strategic response from other oil exporters, would lower oil prices by 14 percent or $10 per barrel in 2016. Oil importers, including the European Union (EU) and United States (US), will gain while oil exporters, especially the Gulf countries, will lose.

Secondly, once sanctions and restrictions on financial transactions are relaxed, Iran's trade, which had both declined in absolute terms and shifted away from Europe towards Asia and the Middle East, will expand. The World Bank estimates that sanctions reduced Iranian exports by $17.1 billion during 2012-14, equivalent to 13.5 percent of total exports in that period. Our analysis suggests that the countries that will see the largest post-sanctions increase in trade with Iran include Britain, China, India, Turkey, and Saudi Arabia.

Thirdly, the Iranian economy, which was in recession for two years, will receive a major boost from increased oil revenues—conservatively estimated at about $15 billion in the first year—and lower trade costs. In addition, there are estimates that Iran holds about $107 billion worth of frozen assets (including LCs and oil exports earnings) overseas, of which an estimated

Timeline of International Sanctions on Iran

- 1979 November - US imposes the first sanctions on Iran, banning imports from Iran and freezing $12bn in assets. 1995 March - US companies are prohibited from investing in Iranian oil and gas and trading with Iran.

- 1996 April - Congress passes a law requiring the US government to impose sanctions on foreign firms investing more than $20m a year in the energy sector.

- 2006 December - The UN Security Council imposes sanctions on Iran's trade in nuclear-related materials and technology and freezes the assets of individuals and companies.

- 2007 October - US announces sweeping new sanctions against Iran, the toughest since 1979. UN Security Council tightens economic and trade sanctions on Tehran.

- 2010 June - UN Security Council imposes a fourth round of sanctions against Iran over its nuclear program, including tighter financial curbs and an expanded arms sanctions. 2011 May and December – the assets of 243 Iranian entities and around 40 more individuals are frozen and visa bans imposed.

- 2012 January - US imposes sanctions on Iran's central bank, for its oil export profits. Iranian threatens to block the transport of oil through the Strait of Hormuz.

- 2012 June - US bans the world's banks from completing oil transactions with Iran, and exempts seven major customers India, South Korea, Malaysia, South Africa, Sri Lanka, Taiwan and Turkey - from economic sanctions in return for their cutting imports of Iranian oil.

- 2012 July - European Union boycott of Iranian oil exports comes into effect.

- 2012 October - Iran's currency, the Rial, falls to a record low against the US dollar, losing about 50% of its value since 2011. EU countries announce further sanctions against Iran focusing on banks, trade and gas imports and freezing assets of individuals and companies that supply Iran with technology.

- 2013 November - Iran agrees to curb uranium enrichment above 5% and give UN inspectors better access in return for about

$7 billion in sanctions relief at talks with the P5+1 group—US, Britain, Russia, China, France and Germany—in Geneva.

- 2015 April - Iran and the EU reach a nuclear framework agreement and set for a final agreement in July 2015 with attendant lifting of the EU and the US sanctions on Iran. 2015 July 14th - The P5+1 group reach an agreement with Iran on limiting Iranian nuclear activity in return for the lifting of sanctions.
- 2015 July 20th - The UN Security Council unanimously approved the July 14th agreement.

Source: International media sources.

$29 billion will be released immediately after sanctions removal. Finally, foreign direct investment (FDI), which had declined by billions of dollars following the tightening of sanctions in 2012, is expected to pick up. There has already been some interest shown by foreign multinationals since the April 2015 framework agreement, especially in the oil and gas sectors. The World Bank expects FDI to eventually increase to about $3 - 3.5 billion in a couple of years, double the level in 2015 but still below the peak in 2003.

In addition to slowing down, the Iranian economy underwent a structural shift during the sanctions era, with the oil, automobile, construction and financial sectors declining the most. As sanctions are lifted, these sectors are likely to see an expansion of output.

All these changes to the economy involve shifting resources from one use to another. The most significant aspect of sanctions relief is that it enables resources to be shifted to where they are more productive, that is, for the economy to produce more efficiently. For example, Iran can now produce and export those goods in which it has a comparative advantage, and import goods in which it does not. In short, sanctions relief can be thought of as an economic windfall to the Iranian economy. The World Bank estimates the size of this windfall as a welfare gain of $13 billion or 2.8 percent of current welfare. Like all windfalls, however, they have to be properly managed in order that they sustainably benefit the population. In particular, as oil revenues enter the economy, the exchange rate will appreciate. While this will make imports cheaper, it will also make non-oil exports less competitive. During the early 2000s, when oil prices were soaring (and sanctions were not restrictive), Iran experienced this phenomenon. Many of the exporting industries suffered. In fact, the only ones that made progress were the petrochemicals and chemicals industries, which received massive subsidies, including subsidies on their consumption of fuel. With the lifting of sanctions, the government of Iran has the opportunity to put in place a policy framework that will enable the economy to make maximum use of this windfall and put the economy on a path of sustained economic growth.

US and European Sanctions Are a Double-Edge Sword

Dmitri Trenin

In the following viewpoint, Dmitri Trenin argues that economic sanctions aren't as clear-cut as they might seem. The author discusses how Western-imposed economic sanctions can help or hinder the country applying the restrictions. He points out that sanctions can hurt businesses that invest or trade with the target country, or sanctions can help stiffen the adversaries resolve. Dmitri Trenin is director of the Carnegie Moscow Center and chairs the research council and the Foreign and Security Policy Program.

As you read, consider the following questions:

1. What tools or markers help when applying sanctions?
2. How effective were the 2014 sanctions imposed on Russia?
3. According to the author, who are the (relative) winners of sanctions?

The United States, Europe and other developed economies, faced with challenging fiscal postures and weak domestic political support for engagement, are increasingly unwilling to pursue foreign policy objectives through the projection of military force.

To compensate, these powers continue to seek to project power through their influence over the global economy (including the

"How effective are economic sanctions?" by Dmitri Trenin, World Economic Forum, February 26, 2015. Reprinted by Permission.

dollar and euro) and through their control over multinational corporations (MNCs) domiciled in their countries.

Recent Western sanctions against Russia signalled the beginning of the first great-power conflict since the end of the Cold War. Their stated goal is to change Russia's policies, though Moscow is convinced that the sanctions are aimed at replacing the existing Russian political regime and holding the country down.

The world has also seen the emergence of Western trade controls in recent years aimed at Iran, Myanmar and Venezuela. Indeed, the US and EU in recent months have come up with new forms of sanctions (e.g. the Treasury Department's Sectoral Sanctions Identifications or "SSI" list). Increasingly, Washington policy- makers see sanctions as the drones of the future—highly targeted weapons that can be deployed to devastating effect.

The West's use of economic levers mirrors the tactics of emerging powers with less powerful militaries. Russia has introduced sanctions towards Georgia, Moldova and Ukraine to prevent their drift to the West, while China has used sanctions against Japan and the Philippines over maritime issues.

Economic sanctions and restrictions are a prime tool of geo-economics and can span from stricter sanitary controls to a full-blown economic blockade. What matters is the size and capacity of the country being sanctioned, and the power of the sanctioning country or international coalition. These tools stand alongside economic incentives such as trade regimes, the use of export credits, tied aid and other forms of sovereign-backed finance.

Applying sanctions is usually a double-edged sword. The country applying sanctions hurts its own businesses that trade with or invest in the target country. US companies have had to stay away from Iran, German machine-builders have had to reduce their exports to Russia, and French shipyards have suffered through the freezing and potential cancellation of the sale of Mistral ships to Russia. Sanctions can also provoke counter-sanctions. In 2014, Russia retaliated against Western measures by banning food imports from the countries that had joined sanctions against Moscow.

The consequences of this trend are evolving, but they potentially include companies' "de-globalization." That is, as companies are increasingly forced to think of themselves as tied to their home governments, they will think twice before investing in certain markets abroad. Other consequences include changes in traditional foreign trade patterns in line with new geopolitical alignments. Faced in 2006 with the Russian wine embargo, Georgia had to look for new markets in the West, where it was headed politically. When in 2014 Russia faced Western sanctions, it accelerated its rapprochement with China, the one major power that refused to condemn its actions and shared Moscow's opposition to US global dominance.

The outcome of these geo-economic campaigns is not a zero-sum game. The stronger economy backed by other forms of power can incur more damage on the target country than it will sustain in return, but it does not always alter the political behaviour of the government to be "punished." Sometimes sanctions can make that behaviour even more problematic. Ironically, the true winner may be a third party that jumps into the opening: European countries in the initial phases of US-Iran sanctions; China in the case of current Western sanctions against Russia; Russia in the case of the post-Tiananmen Western weapons ban on China; Turkey in the situation when EU pressure made Russia abandon its South Stream gas pipeline project.

Politically, sanctions are most effective against friends and allies; in the case of adversaries, they can stiffen their resolve – at least in the short term. The sanctions imposed on Russia in 2014 during the crisis over Ukraine have contributed not just to a surge in Vladimir Putin's popularity but, more importantly, to the growth of Russian patriotism and nationalism. In moments of bravado, the Kremlin even hopes that a long period of sanctions can guarantee political stability in the country for many years (although the downturn in the Russian economy might have the opposite effect).

Whether or not they achieve their objectives, sanctions have great economic impact on target countries: their technological development slows down and their populations grow poorer. This breeds popular resentment, to be sure, but "regime change" is not always the outcome. More liberal regimes, like Slobodan Milosevic's in Serbia, may be swept away, but the harsher ones, like Saddam Hussein's in Iraq, cannot be toppled from the inside. Western-headquartered multinational corporations, even the presumably stronger ones, lose their markets.

The (relative) "winners" of this development are the US/ EU (as long as they maintain sufficient leverage over the global economy to be able to make sanctions "bite"), and China (whose companies are often turned to, when Western firms are barred, and that is most active in supporting its companies in global markets). The "losers" are targets of Western sanctions, such as Russia and Iran, and Western- headquartered MNCs that are relatively disadvantaged, as well as, above all, the multilateral institutions designed to safeguard the free flow of trade and investment, such as the World Trade Organization (WTO), that lose credibility by appearing irrelevant.

Economic Sanctions Are a White-Collar War

Thierry Meyssan

In the following viewpoint, Thierry Meyssan likens the consequences of economic sanctions to war, such as the sanctions levied against Iraq by the UN Security Council that resulted in a million dead civilians. He claims sanctions are a strategy by which the United States and European Union dominate by financial and economic means, and ultimately wage war with the intent to kill. Meyssan is a French journalist and political activist. He is the founder of The Voltaire Network, a Lebanon-based alternative media outlet.

As you read, consider the following questions:

1. Before economic sanctions, what strategies were used to influence a city or state?
2. How can the text of sanction be interpreted?
3. According to the author, what contributed to this "white-collar war?"

In the past, conventional war strategy included the siege of a city or a state. It was used to isolate the enemy, to prevent him from using his resources, to submit him to famine, and finally to gain victory. In Europe, the Catholic church firmly condemned this

"Economic sanctions or the white-collar war," by Thierry Meyssan, Translation Pete Kimberley, Voltaire Network, October 17, 2016. www.voltairenet.org/article193738.html. Reprinted by permission.

tactic as criminal, in that it killed civilians first, and the military forces only afterwards.

Today, conventional wars include economic sanctions, which are used for the same purpose. From 1990 to 2003, the sanctions levied against Iraq by the UN Security Council killed more than a million civilians. In fact, it was a war led by the bankers in the name of the institution whose purpose was supposedly to promote peace.

It is probable that several of the states which voted for these sanctions were not aware of their extent nor their consequences. What is certain is that when some members of the Security Council asked for the sanctions to be lifted, the United States and the United Kingdom opposed the motion, thereby assuming the responsibility for a million dead civlians.

After numerous international civil servants had been fired for their participation in the massacre of a million Iraqi civilians, the United Nations began to think about the manner in which they could make the sanctions more effective in terms of the objectives announced. In other words, to ensure that the sanctions would effect only the political and military sectors, and not civilians. There was talk of targeted sanctions.However, despite much research on the subject, no-one has ever practised sanctions against a state which affected its leaders and not its population.

The effect of sanctions is linked to the interpretation that the governments make of the texts which define them. For example, most of the texts evoke sanctions on products which may be used both by civilians and the military, which leaves plenty of room for interpretation. A rifle may be forbidden for export to a certain state because it can be used for war as well as hunting. But a bottle of water can be drunk by a mother as well as a soldier. Consequently, the same texts—according to the political circumstances and the evolution of the government's will—can lead to extremely different results.

The situation is all the more complicated in that the legal sanctions of the Security Council are augmented by the illegal sanctions of the United States and the European Union. Indeed, while some states or intergovernmental institutions can legally refuse commercial relations with other states, they can not establish unilateral sanctions without waging war.

The term sanction gives the impression that the state which is submitted to them has committed a crime, and that it has been tried before being found guilty. This is true for sanctions decreed by the Security Council, but not those decided unilaterally by the United States and the European Union. These are purely and simply acts of war.

After the war against the British in 1812, Washington created the Office of Foreign Assets Control, which is tasked with waging this white-collar war.

Currently, the main states which are victims of sanctions are not the targets of the United Nations, but exclusively those of the United States and the European Union. They are Syria, Iran and Russia. That is to say the three states which are fighting the jihadists supported by the Western powers.

Most of the sanctions that have been decreed are without direct links to the contemporary war against Syria. The sanctions aimed at Damascus are mainly linked to its support for the Lebanese Hezbollah, and to the asylum granted to the Palestinian Hamas (which has since joined the Muslim Brotherhood, and is now fighting against Syria). The sanctions against Iran were allegedly imposed against its military nuclear programme, even though it was closed down by the Ayatollah Khomeiny thirty years ago. They continue to be levied despite the signature of the 5+1 agreement, which was supposed to resolve this problem, which does not in fact exist. Those levied against Russia sanction the incorporation of Crimea after it had refused the Nazi coup d'état in Kiev, qualified as a democratic revolution by NATO.

The most rigorous sanctions currently levied are those affecting Syria. A report drawn up by the UN Office for the Coordinaton of Humanitarian Affairs in Syria, financed by the Swiss Confederation, and made public four months ago, observes that the US and European interpretation of the texts leads to the deprivation, for the majority of Syrians, of many medical care products and also food resources. A great number of medical products are forbidden, since they are considered to be of double usage, and it is impossible to pay for the importation of food via the international banking system.

Although the situation of the Syrian people is not as catastrophic as that of the Iraqis in the 1990's, it is nonetheless a war waged by the United States and the European Union, by financial and economic means, exclusively against the population living under the protection of the Syrian Arab Republic—with intent to kill.

UN and US Targeted Sanctions Are Sometimes Smart, Sometimes Not

Daniel W. Drezner

In the following excerpted viewpoint, Daniel W. Drezner evaluates literature reviews of targeted sanctions and argues that sometimes they were wisely imposed, but often were not. He examines the development of smart sanctions and questions whether they have helped to solve political problems, or just made situations worse. The author takes a hard look at records of successful sanctions and determines if victory was simply relative. Drezner is a professor of international politics at the Fletcher School of Law and Diplomacy at Tufts University and a nonresident senior fellow at the Brookings Institution. He has published articles in numerous scholarly journals as well as in several newspapers and magazines.

As you read, consider the following questions:

1. According to the author, what are the key principles that play into the development of smart sanctions?
2. In what circumstances are comprehensive sanctions more effective than targeted sanctions?
3. According to the author, what should future research on economic evaluation focus on?

As the negative externalities of comprehensive trade sanctions became apparent in the 1990s, many scholars have advocated

"Sanctions Sometimes Smart: Targeted Sanctions in Theory and Practice," by Daniel W. Drezner, International Studies Association. Reprinted by permission.

for smart sanctions (Weiss 1999; Cortright and Lopez 2002a,b; Brzoska 2003; Wallensteen and Staibano 2005). Ostensibly, smart or targeted sanctions are the precision-guided munitions of economic statecraft. They are designed to hurt elite supporters of the targeted regime, while imposing minimal hardship on the mass public. By altering the material incentives of powerful supporters, the argument runs, these supporters will eventually pressure the targeted government into making concessions.[1] The history of targeted sanctions as a policy tool is, in many ways, a rare success story of fruitful collaboration between scholars, policymakers, and diplomats.[2] The smart sanctions approach has been accepted as an example of "best practices" in both the United Nations and the United States.

This review essay traces the origins and assessments of the targeted sanctions approach. How and why did smart sanctions successfully permeate the foreign policy community? Has this innovation yielded a better approach to the use of economic sanctions? In many ways, smart sanctions represent a classic example of Kingdon's (1984) model of policy innovation. In his work on agenda-setting, Kingdon suggests three "streams" that feed into policy creation: problem recognition, the development of policy alternatives, and the sating of key principals' political incentives. All three of these streams come into play in looking at the development of the smart sanctions framework.

The development of smart sanctions has solved many of the political problems that prior efforts at comprehensive trade sanctions had created. Smart sanctions served as a useful focal point for policy coordination among the great powers, medium powers, and global civil society (Garrett and Weingast 1993). In many ways, these sanctions are smarter. Nevertheless, there is no systematic evidence that smart sanctions yield better policy results vis-à-vis the targeted country. Indeed, in many ways, the smart sanctions framework has been too successful. Recent research suggests that, in some instances, options other than smart sanctions should be pursued. It would behoove policymakers and scholars to look beyond the targeted sanctions framework to examine the conditions under which different kinds of economic statecraft should be deployed.

This essay is divided into five sections. The next section discusses how the Iraq sanctions in the 1990s created a political crisis for comprehensive sanctions. Iraq led to a search for new thinking about economic statecraft. The third section looks at the evolution of targeted sanctions in theory and practice. It explains why smart sanctions emerged as a useful focal point for the integration of scholarship and practice in this area and how it solved the political problems raised by the sanctioning of Iraq. The fourth section evaluates the use of smart sanctions as a policy tool based on the scholarly literature. The final section summarizes and concludes with suggestions for future study of economic statecraft.

[…]

Assessing Smart Sanctions

There are two ways to evaluate the performance of the smart sanctions framework in world politics. First, have smart sanctions ameliorated the humanitarian costs that more comprehensive sanctions create? Second, have targeted sanctions improved target state compliance? The evidence provides moderate support for smart sanctions being more humane but less effective than more comprehensive measures.

Recent research on the impact of economic coercion in the target country would appear to support the humanitarian arguments in favor of smart sanctions. Shagabutdinova and Berejikian (2007) examined HSE's pre-1990 sanctions data and found that financial sanctions were of shorter duration, lessening the suffering from target populations. Wood (2008) analyzed the effect of economic sanctions on state repression using data from 1976 to 2001. He found that comprehensive sanctions were likely to increase repression in authoritarian countries. In bivariate tests, Peksen and Drury (2009) find that the implementation of sanctions triggers drops in democracy and human rights scores in target governments. Peksen (2009) also shows that sanctions lead to a decline in the physical integrity rights of individuals in target countries. Furthermore, the decline in those rights is greater if comprehensive sanctions are imposed rather than targeted sanctions.

These results suggest that, all else equal, targeted sanctions are a more humane policy tool. However, not all else is equal. Paradoxically, there are a number of conditions under which comprehensive sanctions appear to be better at ameliorating suffering in the target country. All of the econometric literature of the past decade agrees that if the target state is a democracy, comprehensive sanctions are more likely to trigger quick concessions (Bolks and Al-Sowayel 2000; Brooks 2002; Allen 2005, 2008b; Lektzian and Souva 2007). The goal of the sanctions episode also matters. If the sender's aim is regime change, then sanctions that impose larger costs have a greater likelihood of success (Dashti-Gibson et al. 1997). Marinov (2005) found that sanctions of any stripe tended to reduce the staying power of the target government; military action, in contrast, increased the duration of the government in power. Major and McGann (2005) argue that there might be instances when sanctioning the "innocent bystanders" in the target country will be more likely to produce target concessions. Most intriguingly, comprehensive sanctions were most useful in bringing about a quicker end to civil wars. Both Gershenson (2002) and Escriba`-Folch (2010) found that comprehensive embargoes were more effective than targeted sanctions at ending intrastate conflicts.

Smart sanctions are less promising in coercing the target government into making concessions. After reviewing the United Nations sanctions during the 1990s, Cortright and Lopez (2002a,b:8) note that "the obvious conclusion is that comprehensive sanctions are more effective than targeted or selective measures. Where economic and social impact have been greatest, political effects have also been most significant." Elliott (2002:171) arrived at a similar conclusion: "with the exception of Libya, the results of

UN targeted sanctions have been disappointing." In their review essay, Tostenson and Bull (2002:402) concluded: "the optimism expressed in some academic circles and among decision makers at national and international levels appears largely unjustified." At a 2010 International Studies Association panel on the topic, many of the scholarly architects of the smart sanctions approach agreed that, compared to comprehensive sanctions, the policy results had been mixed at best.[7]

There are case studies that demonstrate the utility of targeted sanctions. The exemplar case is the sanctions placed on Libya to renounce aiding terrorism, and, later, its weapons of mass destruction programs. That episode, however, also shows the limits of targeted sanctions. A welter of different policy tools were used to get Libya to alter course, including back-channel negotiations, the Proliferation Security Initiative, and the unspoken threat of invasion after Operation Iraqi Freedom. It was the combination of these policy tools—as well as Muhammar Khaddafi's quixotic nature—that led to Libya's acquiescence (Jentleson and Whytock 2005/06). There have been more extensive investigations into the two most common forms of targeted sanctions—arms embargoes and financial statecraft. The results have been underwhelming. Tierney (2005:661) evaluates arms embargoes in civil wars across five criteria for success, including their symbolic impact. He concludes that "much of the impact of UN arms embargoes in civil wars can be summarized as irrelevance or malevolence." Fruchart, Holtom, Wezeman, Strandow, and Wallensteen (2007) reach a similar conclusion. Brzoska (2008) offers a slightly more hopeful assessment. He points to clear successes, such as the 1993–2003 arms embargo of Angola. He also argues that there has been an increasing amount of effectiveness over time in halting the transfer of weapons to armed combatants. Qualifying this result as a "success," however, is problematic. As Damrosch (1994) and Tierney (2005) observe, arms embargoes can have malevolent distributional effects. They reward the actor possessing the largest ex ante cache of weapons—which is often the actor responsible for the most egregious war crimes. Brzoska also acknowledges that, over time, arms embargoes have been less successful in altering the behavior of target countries, working less than 8% of the time. Paradoxically, however, sender country satisfaction with arms embargoes has increased over time—suggesting that the political virtues of smart sanctions trump the policy virtues.

The literature on financial statecraft is somewhat more upbeat. Hufbauer et al. (1990) originally found in bivariate tests that financial sanctions had a better track record of success than trade sanctions. Shagabutdinova and Berejikian (2007) replicated that finding in multivariate tests, confirming that financial sanctions are more effective. These results are based on pre-1990 episodes, however, and principally involve aid cutoffs—it is far from clear whether these results would carry over into modern financial sanctions.[8] There is evidence that financial sanctions have been useful in coercing countries into changing their antimoney laundering rules (Drezner 2007).

It is not clear, however, whether financial statecraft be as successful on issues more highly valued by the target regime, however (Ang and Peksen 2007). Steil and Litan (2006:77) surveyed recent efforts by the United States to use capital market access to force policy changes in Sudan, Russia, and China. They found that all the targeted entities were able to find alternative sources of financing at minimal cost, concluding, "rarely has so powerful a force been harnessed by so many interests with such passion to so little effect." A collaborative effort to examine efforts at monetary statecraft (Andrews 2005:25) reached a similar conclusion: "among the central findings of our study are the substantial impediments to the efficient exercise of monetary power as a deliberate instrument of economic statecraft.... The tools of monetary statecraft... are often too blunt to be effective when they would most be desired and too diffuse to be directed at particular targets without incurring substantial damage."

Looking at particular cases, the evidence suggests that financial sanctions have hurt both the Iranian and North Korean economies

(Eckert 2008; Loeffler 2009). One former Iranian official admitted in late 2008 that the UN sanctions had increased the price of imports anywhere from ten to thirty percent (Maloney 2010:139). In neither case, however, have the financial sanctions led to concessions at the bargaining table. The only economic pressure that appears to have had an effect in either case was China's cutoff of fuel oil to North Korea after that country's first nuclear test (Kahn 2006). As with the arms embargo data, smart financial sanctions have not translated into policy concessions from the target country.

Conclusion

For decades, economic statecraft was thought to be a backwater in international relations scholarship. Since the mid-1990s, however, there has been a remarkable symbiosis between the scholarly and policy communities on the subject. The political and humanitarian disaster of the Iraq sanctions episode led policymakers to search for innovations in the implementation of economic statecraft. At the same time, researchers began to focus on the precise causal mechanisms through which sanctions were supposed to compel change in the target's behavior. Smart sanctions were the resulting alchemy between the scholarly and policymaking communities.

Any assessment of targeted sanctions at this juncture must be labeled as preliminary. States and international organizations have only started moving down the learning curve on implementing sanctions in the past decade (Cortright and Lopez 2002b). Further work is clearly needed. Nevertheless, the evidence to date suggests that smart sanctions are no better at generating concessions from the target state. In many ways, they are worse. They do, however, appear to solve several political problems for sender countries. Because they are billed as minimizing humanitarian and human rights concerns, they receive only muted criticism from global civil society (Craven 2002). Because they do not impede significant trade flows, smart sanctions can be imposed indefinitely with minimal cost. They clearly solve the political problem of "doing something" in the face of target state transgressions. They do not solve the policy problem of coercing the target state into changing its policies.

Future research in this area should focus on two areas. First, more rigorous empirical work is needed on the relative effect of smart sanctions versus more comprehensive sanctions. There are now a sufficient number of smart sanctions cases for statistical analysis. The long-term impact of smart sanctions is worthy of further study—in particular, to see whether their effects are different from sanctions that include a trade component. With the addition of post-Cold War data to the HSE data set (Hufbauer et al. 2007) and the development of the Threat and Imposition of Economic Sanctions (TIES) data set (Morgan et al. 2009), the opportunity exists for more rigorous testing.

Second, and more importantly, the statecraft literature needs to pay greater attention to the burgeoning work on politics in authoritarian countries. The general assumption behind recent sanctions scholarship is that authoritarian leaders are better able to resist economic pressure than democratic states. Clearly, however, authoritarian leaders have domestic constraints that affect their behavior in international crises (Escribà-Folch 2007; Weeks 2008; Escribà-Folch and Wright 2010). Different types of authoritarian countries have different kinds of domestic constraints. The political economy of the Iranian economy is clearly different from North Korea's. A greater theoretical and empirical focus on authoritarian politics would inform both the theory and practice of economic statecraft—and, in the process, illuminate the inner workings of nondemocratic governments.

This review also raises two methodological warnings. One problem with the older generation of sanctions scholarship was the tendency to extrapolate general propositions from high-profile cases (Collier and Mahoney 1996; Drezner 1999). It is worth pondering whether the research on targeted sanctions suffers from a similar problem. Targeted sanctions were first developed in response to Iraq—but Iraq was an extreme outlier on multiple dimensions. Even if policymakers are concerned with big events, Iraq is a dangerous case for inductive generalization.

The research into smart sanctions also suggests the seductive danger of focusing excessively on precise causal mechanisms and process-tracing in the development of policy-relevant research (George and Bennett 2005). Excessive attention to one causal process can blind researcher and policymakers to the possibility that there can be substitutable causal processes at work. Multiple pathways can exist through which an independent policy variable affects the outcome. Consider the possibility, for example, that smart sanctions offer only one causal pathway to success—elite dissatisfaction. If that pathway is blocked by target countermeasures, then smart sanctions will not achieve their desired result. Sanctions that impose greater costs on the target state might offer multiple pathways—mass unrest, elite dissatisfaction, regime change— through which the target government must acquiesce (Drezner n.d.). An appreciation for multiple causal processes would help sanctions scholars avoid the dangerous charge of policy naivité.

Endnotes

1. Consistent with the literature, I refer to the sanctioning actor as the "sender" and the sanctioned actor as the "target."

2. The sender bias of the literature should be stressed at the outset. Implicitly or explicitly, all of this literature is written from the sender's perspective. To my knowledge, there is little to no scholarly work that focuses on how to subvert or weaken sanctions from the target's perspective.

7. "UN Sanctions: A Model of Scholar/Practitioner Collaboration?" roundtable at the International Studies Association annual meeting, New Orleans, LA, February 2010.

8. These results also suffer from omitted variable bias. Aid flows are strongly correlated with alliance relationships, which Shagabutdinova and Berejikian did not include in their regression analysis.

US Travel Bans Define Terrorists

Ibrahim Al-Marashi

In the following viewpoint, Ibrahim al-Marashi evaluates how travel bans and immigration restrictions have influenced the American perception of terrorists. From Nixon to Trump, the use of executive orders to enforce restrictions comes with the human cost of associating Arabs and Muslims with terrorism. Ibrahim al-Marashi is an associate professor in the Department of History at California State University, San Marcos. He is the co-author of Iraq's Armed Forces: An Analytical History; The Modern History of Iraq *(4th ed.); and the forthcoming* A Concise History of the Middle East *(12th ed.).*

As you read, consider the following questions:

1. What was Nixon's travel ban a response to?
2. Before the trend of banning travel from the Middle East, what legislation was used?
3. What was the rational behind Operation Boulder?

On September 24, 2017, President Trump issued a third executive order (termed "Travel Ban 3.0" in the media) restricting travel to the United States as well as the admission of refugees. The restricted countries are now Chad, Iran, Libya, Somalia, Syria, Yemen, Venezuela, and North Korea—the first six of which are Muslim-majority. Since Trump's stated rationale for

"Travel Bans in Historical Perspective: Executive Orders Have Defined 'Terrorists' Since Nixon," by Ibrahim Al-Marashi, American Historical Association, November 2017. Reprinted by Permission.

the measure, first issued on January 27, is protecting Americans, it's worth asking how travel bans and immigration restrictions via executive order have shaped perceptions that Muslims are terrorists.

On the evening of Friday, February 3, 2017, Judge James Robart of the District Court for the Western District of Washington blocked Trump's first executive order suspending immigration from seven Muslim-majority countries, including Iraq, my ancestral home. The next day I drove from my home in northern San Diego County to Los Angeles International Airport to offer translation services to lawyers there. On the way back, stuck in the grueling traffic of Los Angeles, I began to wonder whether there had been an American travel ban directed at Middle Easterners before.

Later that week one of my graduate students, Gretta Ziminsky, informed me that Richard Nixon had set the precedent of banning travel from the Middle East through executive order. (Before Nixon, immigration restrictions targeting Middle Eastern populations had been part of broad pieces of legislation, such as the Immigration Act of 1924.) Trump's fiat is therefore embedded in a deeper American history of conceiving Middle Eastern populations as security threats. Taking Nixon's policy as a starting point, we can see how government attitudes toward Arab and Muslim Americans have changed over time.

My graduate student's MA thesis examines the historical evolution of terrorism in the imagination of American policy elites. We both assumed that these elites saw terrorism as tangential to the superpower rivalry with the USSR, even when left-leaning groups, some of them Soviet proxies, conducted attacks in the Middle East, Europe, and South America. We also assumed that before 9/11, the American government viewed terrorism as an international problem that did not affect the United States.

As I began researching the subject for myself, I found out that the Nixon travel ban was a response to the Palestinian group Black September's attack on Israeli athletes during the Munich Olympics on September 25, 1972. Hours after the attacks, Nixon sent the secretary of state the "Memorandum Establishing a Cabinet

A List of Designated Terrorists

A plethora of international, regional and national lists now span the globe, containing thousands of designated terrorist entities and their perceived and alleged supporters. As well as implementing UN sanctions regimes, a number of UN Security Council Resolutions impose legal obligations on states to institute domestic counterterrorism laws. In addition to criminalising non-state armed groups, political parties, non-government organisations (NGOs), charities, activists, dissidents and others have inevitably been caught in the net, whether listed directly or through association with listed parties. The effects vary according to the applicable legal regime, but the sanctions typically include asset-freezes, travel bans, arms embargoes and the criminalisation of membership and support for banned groups.

"Building Peace in Permanent War", by Ben Hayes, Gavin Sullivan, Louise Boon-Kuo and Vicki Sentas, Transnational Institute, February 16, 2015. Reprinted by Permission.

Committee to Combat Terrorism," which formed a working group that included the State Department, the Secret Service, the Immigration and Naturalization Service, the CIA, and the FBI. The memo charged the working group with drafting new domestic and foreign anti-terrorism policies.[1]

With a set of directives code-named Operation Boulder, the working group stepped up the vetting of visa applicants from the Middle East in US embassies abroad and in Washington, and monitored Arabs and Arab Americans domestically. According to legal scholar Susan Akram, Operation Boulder was "perhaps the first concerted US government effort to target Arabs in the US for special investigation with the specific purpose of intimidation, harassment, and to discourage their activism on issues relating to the Middle East."[2]

This was the first US government policy carrying the implication that all Arabs were potential terrorists. Although government documents don't explicitly detail the origin and evolution of this view, Akram argues that negative stereotypes in American popular culture and news media, as well as lobbying by pro-Israel groups, all played a role.[3] It is also unclear just how the administration settled on travel restrictions as the means of preventing terrorism in the United States, when there were no indications that Black September or other Middle Eastern groups planned to target Americans within the country's borders.

Nonetheless, by April 1974, officials understood that the rationale behind Operation Boulder was to monitor Arab travelers, especially Palestinians (including refugees among them). That month the State Department issued a memo reading, in part, "In light of the obvious and continuing threat from potential Arab terrorists, particularly Palestinians, none of the agencies in the Working Group wishes to eliminate Operation Boulder at this time." Palestinians were thus a security threat, even though the US was not expecting a major influx of Palestinians.[4]

The memo, however, did highlight criticisms of Operation Boulder emerging within the State Department. There were problems keeping up with the operation's demands, including extra paperwork required to vet visa applicants in Middle Eastern embassies and in Washington. About 40 to 50 visa applicants per day were vetted, and only 23 visas were denied during the program's run.[5] The memo also argued that revising vetting procedures would repair America's image in the Middle East: "day-to-day relations with Arab countries will be improved at a time when an improvement would be particularly beneficial." Nevertheless, the FBI objected to modifying the process, and the State Department deferred to its concerns.

The Nixon-era measures also monitored Arab Americans domestically.[6] The American Civil Liberties Union wrote to the attorney general on February 8, 1974, criticizing Operation Boulder as unfairly targeting "ethnic Arabs who were so defined on the basis of a person's parentage" and painting the whole endeavor as a "fishing expedition" to gather information, violating the First, Fourth, and Fifth Amendments.[7]

The letter documents FBI agents accusing Arabs of belonging to terrorist organizations as "an investigative tactic" that would "elicit the subject's cooperation by scaring him or her." Immigration authorities approached Arab students in the United States, questioned them about their political beliefs, and required them to sign affidavits that they would not engage in political activities. Selective application of technicalities in immigration and naturalization laws were used to deport Arabs.[8] The Munich attack hardly figured in defenses of these tactics; instead, they were justified in vague language as combating terrorism. This shift in conceiving the problem was likely influenced by tensions after the 1973 Arab-Israeli War.

The FBI eventually terminated Operation Boulder in 1975 after questioning its effectiveness.[9] But the conflation of Arabs and terrorists was accomplished. Nixon's executive response to Black September strained government resources, alienated Middle Eastern states and Arab Americans, and achieved little. But a precedent had been established.

With the Iranian hostage crisis of 1979, the administration of Jimmy Carter canceled visas issued to Iranians and monitored those already in the country.[10] But the protean threat of Al-Qaida presented a singular challenge because it was a transnational, nonstate actor. Where Carter had targeted a single nationality, which included not only Muslims but also Iranian Jews, Christians, and members of the Baháʼí religion, the aftermath of the attacks of September 11, 2001, represented a throwback to Nixon-era measures that blurred the distinction between international and domestic security. Of course, the George W. Bush administration used force against Afghanistan when Taliban leaders refused to turn in Osama bin Laden, but in 2002 it also initiated the National Security Entry-Exit Registration System (NSEERS), targeting Muslim immigrants as potential terrorists.

It is now mostly the Islamic State of Iraq and Syria that is perceived as a protean threat to the "homeland." Barack Obama disbanded NSEERS as a failure in 2016, but Trump's election has reinvigorated efforts to target Muslim citizens, immigrants, and travelers as potential domestic terrorists. While on the campaign trail, Trump responded to the Paris attacks of November 2015 by declaring that he would create a database to register Muslims in the United States, and after the San Bernardino attack in December, he vowed to impose a "Muslim ban." Trump's first executive order targeted travelers from seven nations without specifying a religious test, but the fact that these countries were predominantly Muslim raised suspicions within and beyond Muslim communities in the United States. Unlike George W. Bush, who repeatedly stressed that the United States was not at war with Islam, Trump did not make this distinction successfully.

In response to terrorist attacks in Europe, Nixon and Trump rapidly issued security measures, perhaps not noticing terrorist attacks against civilians within the Middle East because they commanded smaller headlines. Refugees suffered as a result of belonging to groups deemed security threats: Palestinians then, Syrians today. As we wait for a Supreme Court ruling on the new executive order's constitutionality, we should keep its historical precedents in mind, as well as the human costs of associating Arabs and Muslims with terrorism. The complaints lodged in 1974 resonate with the situation they might face in 2017—and beyond.

Endnotes

1. "Memorandum Establishing a Cabinet Committee to Combat Terrorism," September 25, 1972, http://www.presidency.ucsb.edu/ws/?pid=3596.
2. Susan M. Akram, "The Aftermath of September 11, 2001: The Targeting of Arabs and Muslims in America," Arab Studies Quarterly 24, no. 2/3 (Spring/Summer 2002): 68.
3. Akram, "The Aftermath of September 11, 2001."
4. "Memorandum from the Special Assistant to the Secretary of State and Coordinator for Combating Terrorism (Hoffacker) to the Deputy Undersecretary for Management (Brown)," Washington, April 23, 1974, https://history.state.gov/historicaldocuments/frus1969-76ve03/d214.
5. Yazan al-Saadi, "Revisiting US-Arab Diplomacy: Operation Boulder and the Oil Embargo," Al-Akhbar, April 8, 2013, http://english.al-akhbar.com/node/15474.
6. Nadine Naber, "Arab Americans and US Racial Formations," in Amaney Jamal and Nadine Naber, Race and Arab Americans Before and After 9/11: From Invisible Citizens to Visible Subjects (Syracuse, NY: Syracuse University Press, 2007), 34.

Economic Sanctions

7. American Civil Liberties Union, "Operation Boulder," February 8, 1974, https://declassifiedboulder.files.wordpress.com/2013/04/detroitletter.pdf.
8. ACLU, "Operation Boulder."
9. Al-Saadi, "Revisiting US-Arab Diplomacy."
10. Jimmy Carter, "Sanctions against Iran Remarks Announcing US Actions," American Presidency Project, April 7, 1980, http://www.presidency.ucsb.edu/ws/?pid=33233.

Periodical and Internet Sources Bibliography

The following articles have been selected to supplement the diverse views presented in this chapter.

British Broadcasting Corporation News, "Trump's Executive Order: Who Does Travel Ban Affect?" February 10, 2017. http://www .bbc.com/news/world-us-canada-38781302.

Rick Gladstone and David E. Sanger, "Security Council Tightens Economic Vise on North Korea, Blocking Fuel, Ships and Workers," *New York Times*, December 22, 2017. https://www .nytimes.com/2017/12/22/world/asia/north-korea-security -council-nuclear-missile-sanctions.html.

Borja Guijarro-Usobiaga, "Economic Sanctions: Past & Future," London School of Economic and Political Science, April 16, 2015. http://eprints.lse.ac.uk/76602.

Harvard University Press, "The Most Crippling Sanctions in the History of Sanctions," October 16, 2012. http://harvardpress .typepad.com/hup_publicity/2012/10/the-most-crippling -sanctions-in-the-history-of-sanctions.html.

Adrian Hearn, "Beyond Big Cigars and Vintage Cars," *Public Affairs*, University of Melbourne, April 4, 2016. https://pursuit.unimelb .edu.au/articles/beyond-big-cigars-and-vintage-cars.

Ralph Jennings, "North Korea Is Looking at Bitcoin to Escape Its Crippling Economic Sanctions," *Forbes*, December 19, 2017. https://www.forbes.com/sites/ralphjennings/2017/12/19 /north-korea-seeks-a-pile-of-bitcoin-to-escape-economic -sanctions/#130696d039ba.

Norwich University, "Do Economic Sanctions Work?" https:// graduate.norwich.edu/resources-mair/infographics-mair/do -economic-sanctions-work.

Amy Pereira, "Do Sanctions Work?" Economics Student Society of Australia, October 6, 2017. http://economicstudents .com/2017/10/do-sanctions-work.

Francisco Rodríguez, "Why More Sanctions Won't Help Venezuela," *Foreign Policy*, January 12, 2018. http://foreignpolicy .com/2018/01/12/why-more-sanctions-wont-help-venezuela.

Kenneth Rogoff, "Economic Sanctions Have a Long and Chequered History," *Guardian*, January 5, 2015. https://www.theguardian

.com/business/2015/jan/05/economic-sanctions-long-history
-mixed-success.

Andrew S. Weiss, "The Role of Sanctions in US-Russian Relations,"
Carnegie Endowment for International Peace, July 11, 2016.
http://carnegieendowment.org/2016/07/11/role-of-sanctions-in
-u.s.-russian-relations-pub-64056.

CHAPTER 2

Efficacy of Economic Sanctions

Sanctions Are Outside of International Law

James A. Paul

In the following viewpoint, James A. Paul takes a critical eye to economic sanctions, and argues that rather than accurately enforcing law they may themselves be outside of law. He looks at sanctions of the past for answers, such as the Cuba embargo and the debate of Iraq sanctions. Paul is a writer, consultant and editor, and he long served as a non-profit executive with special expertise on international affairs, the United Nations, and the Middle East. He has written 150 articles, given many lectures, and provided more than 1,500 interviews to the media.

As you read, consider the following questions:

1. How do economic sanctions impose hardship outside of the targeted country?
2. According to a survey of sanctions, which state is the primary initiator of sanctions?
3. What were the effects of the Cuba embargo?

M ost people consider sanctions a peaceful and effective means to enforce international law. Under Article 41 of the UN Charter, the Security Council may call on Member States "to apply measures not involving the use of armed force to give effect to its decisions." Typically, sanctions cut off trade and investments, preventing a target country from buying or selling goods in the global marketplace. Sanctions may aim at particular items like arms or oil. They may cut off air traffic, suspend or drastically curtail diplomatic relations, block movement of persons, bar investments, or freeze international bank deposits.

Sanctions enjoy a good reputation that many now question. Increasingly, critics charge that sanctions are cruel, unfair and even violent. International law has developed no standards on which sanctions can be based or the destructive impact of sanctions limited. Ironically, then, sanctions are used to enforce law, but themselves are outside of the law.

Suffering of the Innocent

Sanctions impose hardship—affecting ordinary people, far more than leaders. In Supplement to An Agenda for Peace, published in January 1995, Secretary General Boutros Ghali called sanctions "a blunt instrument." "They raise the ethical question of whether suffering inflicted on vulnerable groups in the target country is a legitimate means of exerting pressure on political leaders whose behavior is unlikely to be affected by the plight of their subjects." In a Security Council debate on January 19, 1995, Amb. Nihal Rodrigo of Sri Lanka concurred, saying that decisions must take better account of the sanctions' impact on ordinary people and must seek to avoid the "suffering of the innocent."

As evidence has accumulated on the harsh effects of sanctions, particularly in Iraq, experts have increasingly recognized this negative side of sanctions and questioned whether human suffering can be justified by the original purpose.

Collateral Damage

Sanctions also cause hardship outside the target country, in what is known (borrowing from military terminology) as "collateral damage." Sanctions invariably hurt countries that are neighbors or major trading partners, who lose export markets, government revenues, and employment opportunities. Sanctions may harm big business interests and they tend to cause suffering among the poorest and most vulnerable.

Article 50 of the UN Charter directly addresses the right of countries to appeal for financial assistance as compensation for their losses when sanctions are applied. The Secretary General in his 1995 report called for urgent action to respond to this problem, saying that the costs of sanctions "should be borne equitably by all Member States and not exclusively by the few who have the misfortune to be neighbors or major economic partners of the target country." In the January 1995 Council debate, Amb. Danilo Turk of Slovenia argued along the same lines that a disproportionate burden of sanctions is borne by neighboring states and trading partners and he argued for "statements of impact assessment" so that burdens could be more equitably shared.

Double Standards, Changing Rules

Critics argue that sanctions are too often imposed unfairly, using standards that are unevenly applied or biased. The whims or interests of the mighty—and not clear rules of international law—too often determine the targets of sanctions and the harshness of the sanction regimes. Sanctions, argued Amb. Joseph Legwaila of Botswana, are meant to bring about a "change of behavior," they are not supposed to be "punishment or retribution." When sanctions were imposed on Iraq to induce its withdrawal from occupied Kuwait, sceptics pointed out that many other invasions and occupations had not resulted in sanctions. Israel, Morocco, Turkey and Indonesia, for example, all avoided sanctions when they invaded neighbors. If the Security Council wants its sanctions to be seen as legitimate, it should impose them more consistently, critics argue.

Once UN sanctions are in place, they are supervised by a "sanctions committee" of the Security Council, which operates secretively and cannot be monitored and made accountable to the public. This makes the ongoing sanctions process highly politicised and very open to pressure from Permanent Members. Sanctions may begin with one justification and continue with others. The Secretary General in his 1995 report mentioned this kind of problem: "The objectives . . . have not always been clearly defined. Indeed, they may sometimes seem to change over time. This combination of imprecision and mutability makes it difficult for the Security Council to agree on when . . . sanctions can be lifted."

Elusive but Occasional Success

For all the pain they impose, sanctions usually do not succeed. There is a long history of failure to prove it. League of Nations sanctions, imposed in 1935, failed to force Italy to pull out of Ethiopia. More recently, UN sanctions have failed to induce Libya to turn over two citizens for trial in the Lockerbie airliner bombing, or to induce Iraq to substantially modify its policies. Unilateral sanctions, imposed by a single state, are even more likely to fizzle. The United States grain embargo against the Soviet Union in 1980 did not produce a Soviet withdrawal from Afghanistan, nor have the long and punishing sanctions by the United States against Cuba resulted in political change on that island. Sanctions are often ignored by some governments or circumvented by traders chasing a high profit margin. Unilateral sanctions can even backfire, harming exporters in the sanction-imposing country most of all. In the 1980 grain embargo, US farmers suffered more than Soviet consumers.

The UN Security Council imposed only two sanctions regimes in its first forty-five years. Surprisingly enough, both are generally considered effective. They targeted Southern Rhodesia (now Zimbabwe) and South Africa, both white-only settler regimes. The Security Council imposed its first mandatory sanctions on Rhodesia in 1966 following the white minority's unilateral declaration of independence. The Council finally lifted the sanctions in 1979, after negotiations led to a black government.

Britain and the United States opposed sanctions against apartheid South Africa, in spite of strong pressures in the Security Council. Finally, after weak "voluntary" measures (voted in 1963) had little result, Britain and the US agreed to a Council-imposed mandatory arms embargo in 1977. Efforts to toughen sanctions through the UN met with further Anglo-American opposition, including a draft resolution vetoed by both permanent members on March 8, 1988 (S/19585). But nevertheless, an international campaign, induced private investors and governments to adopt sanctions measures. In 1989, the campaign finally succeeded in pushing a sanctions bill through the US Congress, against the oppositon of the administration. Thoughout, shippers, especially big oil companies, often flouted the embargoes. But thanks to the international campaign, maritime and longshore unions, along with United Nations agencies, helped enforce the sanctions by exposing sanction-breakers to public scrutiny. Many believe that the sanctions helped force the apartheid regime to finally capitulate, in a relatively peaceful transition of power. Whatever hardship the sanctions imposed on both Zimbabwe and South Africa, the outcome seems to have been well worth it.

An influential study argues that of 116 cases of sanctions imposed between 1914 and 1990, between a quarter and a third resulted in some policy change in the target country. The likelihood of "success," concluded the authors, decreases as the goals of sanctions become more general and "ambitious."

Who Has Applied Sanctions?

The survey of sanctions found that the United States was the primary initiator of sanctions—in about 70 percent of the cases. A third of the cases were unilateral sanctions and most of the rest were ad hoc coalitions. Only 12 percent of all sanctions were applied in a truly collective manner.

How Deep Do Sanctions Really Bite?

Because sanction regimes are so different, their impact on the target economies is quite various. Experts say that partial sanctions may reduce GNP by 1% or so and that major sanctions, like those imposed on South Africa, probably reduce GNP by up to 5%. These modest effects show why sanctions so often fail. But they

Let's Admit That Sanctions Are a Failure

The U.S. financial system is the engine of all global trade. Sanctions that are prohibitive or otherwise too restrictive to foster trade risks driving business to foreign markets — and, in doing so, broker new alliances between longtime American friends and foes.

"It is important to make sure our sanctions tools remain effective and are not overused," acting U.S. Treasury Undersecretary Adam Szubin said this month. "We must continue to balance the costs and benefits of our sanctions regime in our favor."

Szubin oversees the Treasury Department's counterterrorism and financial intelligence arm. His boss, Treasury Secretary Jack Lew, warned Congress in March that financial transactions may bypass the United States if sanctions "make the business environment too complicated or unpredictable, or if they excessively interfere with the flow of funds worldwide.

"We must be conscious of the risk that overuse of sanctions could undermine our leadership position within the global economy, and the effectiveness of the sanctions themselves," Lew said.

Tensions wrought by U.S. sanctions against Russia and Ukrainian separatists, for example, have divided U.S. allies in Europe that were already financially struggling before being hit with the economic penalties' knock-on effects. On Thursday, the lower house of France's parliament voted in a nonbinding agreement to lift EU sanctions against Russia.

"Sanctions have been a success? No. It's a true failure," Italian lawmaker Deborah Bergamini, who is also a delegate to the Parliamentary Assembly of the Council of Europe, told a Rome forum in February that pondered the West's relations with Russia. She said Italy has lost at least 1.25 billion euros in exports since U.S. and European Union sanctions were imposed in 2014.

"'Sanctions Are a Failure…Let's Admit That,'" by David Francis and Lara Jakes, Foreign Policy, April 28, 2016.

seem to contradict reports of serious human suffering in target countries. In fact, a GNP decline of 5% in a poor country is likely to result in considerable hardship for the poorest people, especially if food imports are cut. Reduction in imports of medicines and vaccines can also create great hardship and suffering, even though a relatively small proportion of overall GNP is at stake.

In the final analysis, sanctions must be measured in terms of who they effect, in what way and with what final result. Greatly increased disease, malnutrition, and mortality in the target country are results that cannot easily be defended against world public opinion. Sanctions that have such results are likely to lose credibility and eventually collapse.

A Flurry of Recent Sanctions

The Security Council imposed its third set of sanctions on Iraq in 1990 and followed with a number of others: former Yugoslavia (1991), Libya, Somalia, Haiti and Angola (1993), Rwanda (1994), Liberia (1995), Sudan and Burundi (1996). Some of these recent sanctions regimes have attracted sharp criticism, especially the sanctions against Libya and Iraq. Canada's distinguished international lawyer Geoffrey Grenville-Wood wrote in a 1993 article that the sanctions against Libya to force extradition of two suspects in an aircraft bombing was "spurious and ill-founded," since the Council was wrong in claiming international peace and security were threatened. Did France agree to hand over its agent that blew up a Greenpeace ship in New Zealand, Grenville-Wood asked.

With so many sanctions in force, debates about sanctions at the UN have intensified. Scarcely any country is not affected by sanctions to some degree and several dozen have suffered severe trade disruption and economic pain. As a result, the issue of sanctions now arises in many UN forums throughout the year.

Sanctions Against Iraq

Over the course of more than seven years of sanctions against Iraq, several UN agencies and human rights organizations have produced reports showing malnutrition due to blockage of food, severe health problems due to absence of medicines and water purification systems. Some observers have argued that the sanctions policies have been imposed primarily in order to regulate the world's supply (and price) of oil, rather than to change the policies of the target state. This argument seems plausible, but it is difficult to prove. Sanctions experts agree, though, that in general there are often hidden reasons behind the nominal legalities used to justify sanctions.

As time has passed, the humanitarian emergency in Iraq has deepened. Evidence has emerged that the United States and Britain, through their role in the UN Security Council, have blocked shipments to Iraq of harmless but vital goods, ranging from medicines to sewage treatment facilities, clearly damaging public health. The UN sanctions committee on Iraq has been hostage to political pressures that have caused great suffering, widespread malnutrition and many tens of thousands of unnecessary deaths—perhaps more than during the actual Gulf War hostilities in 1991. The great majority of countries now oppose these sanctions, even if many countries remain sharply critical of the regime of Saddam Hussein.

The Cuba Embargo

The unilateral United States trade embargo of Cuba, in force since 1962, provides evidence of an even more repugnant sanctions regime, which is opposed by a large majority of the world's countries and regularly condemned in the UN General Assembly. The embargo has done harm to the Cuban economy and made travel between the US and Cuba difficult and costly. Even governments that are decidedly unenthusiastic about Cuban President Fidel Castro consider the embargo illegal and see it as unfairly punishing ordinary Cubans. After the UN General Assembly overwhelmingly passed a resolution condemning the US embargo in 1995 for the fourth straight year (A/50/10), the Secretary General wrote to governments and agencies asking for information that could be incorporated into a report. By 5 September, 60 countries and 5 agencies had responded. The responses were all critical of the embargo. This information can be found in a UN document

(A/51/355).

Over the years, the United States has imposed many unilateral political and trade sanctions, often to punish "enemies" or win economic advantages. Usually the government justifies sanctions in legal or moral terms—the target countries are said to "violate" something sacred like "human rights" "democracy" and "fair trade." But often there are less elevated but more economically compelling reasons, such as the drive to control oil reserves and other natural resources. Invariably the sanctions are imposed unilaterally because they would not win support in multilateral bodies. This kind of sanction may now encounter stronger opposition internationally under the rules of the World Trade Organization.

The US Helms-Burton Act of 1996 has imposed penalties on third parties doing business in Cuba, bringing sharp protests from Canada, Mexico, European countries and many others. The European Union is planning a formal protest to the WTO. On June 4, 1996, the General Assembly of the Organization of American States passed a resolution asking for a legal opinion on the embargo from the Inter American Juridical Committee. The Committee returned an opinion that Helms-Burton "is not in conformity with international law." This opinion was sent to the United Nations on September 18, 1996. On November 12, 1996, the UN General Assembly passed a resolution again condemning the embargo by the largest vote ever—117 ayes, 3 nays and 38 abstentions. All the European Union countries voted in the affirmative, as did Canada. The new resolution contained language sharply critical of the Helms-Burton law.

Think Tank Studies and UN Assessments

Interest in sanctions has grown at various universities, think tanks and NGOs. When the Security Council began imposing sanctions, a rising tide of US foundation grants funded a number of projects— at Notre Dame, the Carnegie Commission on Preventing Deadly Conflict, the Carter Center, the Council on Foreign Relations, Brown University, the National Academy of Sciences and the Center for Economic and Social Rights. Some of these studies considered sanctions solely as a US policy tool, while others were deeply concerned about broader humanitarian implications. The Notre Dame Project produced the influential volume *Economic Sanctions.* Meanwhile, UN agencies commissioned studies, including a major project by the Department of Humanitarian Affairs, undertaken by German scholars. The General Assembly Working Group on Agenda for Peace set up a sub-group on sanctions, chaired by Amb. Amorim of Brazil.

UN staff have also written about sanctions. James Ngobi, Secretary of the Security Council Sanctions Committees, noted in an influential 1995 article that Council-imposed sanctions are rarely imposed swifty or decisively enough, they depend on implementation by member states (which in practice is uneven), they lack punitive measures against sanction-breakers, and they lack means to alleviate suffering of affected innocent people.

Call for Monitoring and a Rule-Based Use of Sanctions

The Secretary General returned to the issue of sanctions in his report on Humanitarian Crises, released on 15 July 1995 (A/50/203). Urging the Security Council and the international community to address root causes in order to head off the conflicts, he called attention to the potential of sanctions for creating deeper social distress. "Action taken by the international community to end oppression or bring about change by non-military means," he said, "can have major ramifications for those who are already victimized by inequitable political and economic structures. Economic sanctions hit the poor hardest and can have a deleterious impact on the work of humaniarian organizations."

The critics of sanctions found a powerful ally in the International Red Cross, a highly respected and traditionally non-political body. In its 1995 World Disasters Report, the Red Cross highlighted its growing concern over sanctions' humanitarian impact. The Red Cross President, addressing the General Assembly on 28 November

1995 mentioned his special concern about the situation in Iraq and said that "the high price paid by the most vulnerable groups of the population is apparent." He went on to call for "a formal mechanism" to "assess the potential impact of sanctions and monitor their effect."

In January of 1996, the Secretary General presented another report to the Security Council, asking it to reconsider the impact of sanctions. He pointed out that sanctions may greatly set back development and that sanctions can impede or even block the work of humanitarian relief organizations. He called for more precise definitions of the goal of sanctions and the conditions under which they may be lifted. And he warned that under certain conditions sanctions can defeat their own purpose by "provoking a patriotic response against the international community, symbolized by the United Nations, and by rallying the population behind the leaders whose behavior the sanctions are intended to modify."

Targeting Sanctions

Many experts believe that targeted sanctions can be more humanitarian and more effective. Targeting implies sanctions that deliver pressure where it is most effective. Arms embargoes are one type that is commonly used. Another type seeks to hit key groups most severely—like the business or political elite. These groups have a major voice in policy making and they are unlikely to suffer bodily harm from sanctions, even if their standard of living is seriously reduced. Sanctions targeted at these groups may block international travel, embargo luxury imports, and (most effectively) seize foreign bank accounts. Unfortunately, banking and business interests vigorously oppose this kind of sanction. As the *New York Times* reported in March 1996, Britain, France and Germany are "traditionally reluctant to take any action that might damage their position as international financial centers." The *Times* could well have added the United States and Switzerland to the list. Banks simply do not want to give up information on their private accounts and they are nervous about the wider implications of "political" interference in their relations with their customers. For reasons such as these, sanctions that target individual assets are very rarely considered.

In the fall of 1997, after considerable debate, the Security Council decided to impose targetted sanctions on the leadership of the Unita rebel group in Angola. The sanctions mainly consisted of bans on travel for those identified as in top leadership positions, including the rebel chief, Jonas Savimbi. But the Council extended a sanction deadline set for late September.

Who Enforces Sanctions?

Sanctions often fail because they are not enforced. The United Nations has no means to enforce sanctions in its own right. It must depend on compliance by member states and by traders and businesses. If they refuse to comply, then there is no means to impose penalties or bring them to justice. In many recent sanctions, the UN scarcely has had any monitoring capacity. So sanction-busting has flourished.

The UN actually had one effective monitoring system, developed for its sanctions against South Africa. An office in the Centre on Transnational Corporations, linked to a wide network of monitoring sources, kept track of trade and investments in the apartheid state. Each year the Centre issued a major report, causing serious public criticism of governments and businesses. The permanent members seem keen to avoid a repetition of this embarrassment. Instead they prefer the UN to contract out its monitoring and assessment to one or more powerful states. The United States often acts as the enforcer, only deepening suspicions that sanctions are unfair instruments of great powers.

The Debate Over Iraq

The clash over sanctions took a dramatic form in mid-1996. Well into the sixth year of the sanctions on Iraq—sanctions that had been originally imposed under very different circumstances—many countries called for the Security Council to lift its trade embargo, on the grounds that it was causing too much human suffering. The United States and Britain blocked this initiative and insisted on harsh conditions and a limited deal, that would allow the country to sell oil in exchange for food, medicines and other vital necessities under strict UN control. The Iraqi government was at first not willing to accept these conditions. Finally, after a deal was proposed in April 1996, Baghdad's position softened. Pressure on the United States and Britain intensified after a report was issued by the New York-based Center for Economic and Social Rights on 18 May detailing the human suffering caused by the sanctions, as reported by an investigative team of 24 experts from 8 countries. With a green light from the US and Britain, Baghdad signed an agreement with the UN on 20 May, allowing for the sale of $2 billion in Iraqi oil over a six-month period.

Planning for implementation went forward. But on 31 July, the United States government announced that it would oppose the agreement. There was fury in the Security Council where everyone knew that the United States had itself originally set conditions for the agreement. Amb. Tono Eitel of Germany, Chairman of the Council Sanctions Committee on Iraq, told *New York Times* reporter Barbara Crossette he was "troubled and very sad" over the US action. Observers speculated that US electoral politics had caused the last-minute shift. On August 7, the US changed course and finally gave its formal agreement. Shortly afterwards, however, Iraq's government moved troops into a Kurdish zone in the north. Again, the United States and Britain insisted that the sanctions would have to stay in place.

After intense pressure from Council members and others, the US agreed to yet another deal, that was anounced on November 25, allowing $2 billion in oil sales during a six-month period. Many thought the agreement was strongly conditioned by multinational oil companies. As the *New York Times* reported, citing "oil analysts," under conditions of strong demand and low reserves at refineries, Iraqi sales "are likely to only slightly reduce the cost of a barrel of oil on world markets."

Burundi and Sudan

The debate over sanctions in the summer of 1996 extended to Burundi, where the Council imposed a new regime in July due to a coup d'etat and deteriorating inter-ethnic conflict. Given the povery of the country, there was serious doubt about the effect of the sanctions. On August 6, the World Food Programme announced that the Burundi sanctions were preventing humanitarian aid from entering the country, threatening the well being of hundreds of thousands of people. WFP warned that the cut-off of emergency food, medicine and fuel may exacerbate ethnic tensions. At about the same time, the UN Department of Humanitarian Affairs dispatched a 5-person mission to Burundi to examine the consequences of sanctions and the mission was at first blocked from the country because of sanctions-imposed barriers to air travel in neighboring Kenya.

The Council has also faced criticism on its Sudan sanctions, likewise imposed in 1996. The Sudan sanctions are similar to the Libyan sanctions, for they are designed to force the Sudanese government to turn over alleged criminals—in this case people who allegedly attempted to assassinate President Mubarak of Egypt. International lawyers insist that this goes beyond the proper bounds for the Council's action and that it undermines the system of extradition treaties. Sudan's economy is already in very great difficulty, critics point out. Sanctions make matters worse and seem certain to impose hardships that will not be justified.

Broad Debate at the UN

Feelings run high on sanctions at the UN. Many delegations have made heated comments on the issue in 1995 and 1996—in the General Assembly, the Charter Committee, the Sixth (Legal) Committee, the Fifth (Finance) Committee, the Security Council and other bodies. The special sub-group of the Working Group on an Agenda for Peace has considered the question at length.

Delegations are insisting on a better monitoring, a more targeted and humanitarian approach, and real burden-sharing.

But their opinions are purely advisory. So far, not a dime has been allocated through the UN to help share the burden of trading partners. Nor have targeted sanctions come into general use. Nor has monitoring markedly improved. The Security Council remains in control and permanent members seem intent on following past practices. They prefer not to be burdened with rules and they do not want to be billed for collateral damage.

Iraq Sanctions: the latest turn of the Crisis

On October 28, 1996, UNICEF head Carol Bellamy held a news conference about the crisis in Iraq. She said that 4,500 children are dying every month of hunger and disease because of conditions imposed by the sanctions. Yasushi Akashi, Under Secretary General for Humanitarian Affairs said that nations were not contributing to emergency relief funds because they thought that the embargo was soon to be lifted. Other experts noted that Iraq's water and sewage system is crumbling, leading to greater risk of infectious disease. The World Food Programme announced that 180,000 children under the age of 5 in Iraq are malnourished. In an October 29 article on the subject, the New York Times reported that "The standoff over the oil sales has annoyed other diplomats on the Council who say repeated American efforts to stall the plan make sanctions appear unduly harsh and harmful to the most innocent Iraqis."

On December 9, the UN signed another deal that had been announced on November 25. Secretary General Boutros-Ghali said "This is a victory for the poorest of the poor in Iraq, for the women, the children, the sick and the disabled." And Security Council President Paolo Fulci of Italy said when announcing the deal: "More than 20 million innocent Iraqi civilians will be finally saved from starvation and untold suffering . . . anaesthesia will be finally available for surgery . . . four out of ten new born children will no longer die before they reach age one." The following day, there were reports that oil had started to flow. Many weeks will pass before the oil is actually delivered to buyers and the payments are translated into food and other humanitarian supplies. It remains to be seen whether another crisis will erupt and block the deal as has happened before. Or whether at long last the deal will work and the suffering in Iraq will ease.

Which Way for Sanctions

What way ahead for sanctions? Sanctions advocates would argue that they still hold great promise. But only under conditions of wide international agreement, clear legal basis and purpose, and minimal harm to the innocent. These seem elusive goals in a world where a few powerful states and private interests use sanctions for their own geo-strategic and economic gains. Even so, sanctions continue to offer interesting possibilities. The breadth and intensity of the UN discussions suggests that many delegations (and many NGOs) think sanctions can someday be made to work.

Sanctions Against Zimbabwe Were Unsuccessful and Harmful

Cynthia Chipanga and Torque Mude

In the following excerpted viewpoint, Cynthia Chipanga and Torque Mude conduct an analysis of the effectiveness of sanctions as a law enforcement tool in Zimbabwe. Investigations into travel bans, asset freezes, and arm embargoes reveal sanctions were easily circumvented. Chipanga holds a Bachelors of Arts in International Affairs from Midlands State University in Zimbabwe. Mude was a PhD fellow of Literature and Philosophy in International Politics at the University of South Africa. He is a Social Sciences lecturer at Midlands State University.

As you read, consider the following questions:

1. How has globalization affected sanctions in Zimbabwe?
2. How did economic sanctions affect innocent civilians?
3. According to the authors, who is responsible for the failure of sanctions imposed on Zimbabwe?

International law is an instrument governing the behaviour of states and non state actors in the international system. The main function of international law is to ensure peace and security in the international community. International law consists of law

Chipanga, C., & Mude, T. (2015). An Analysis of the Effectiveness of Sanctions as a Law Enforcement Tool in International Law: A Case Study of Zimbabwe from 2001 to 2013. Open Journal of Political Science, 5, 291-310. 10/21/2015. https://file.scirp.org/pdf/OJPS_2015102114012116.pdf.

enforcement tools that assist in the regulation of the behaviour of international actors. The use of force though not prohibited is usually not the desired way of regulating international actors' behavior; hence the use of sanctions is desired often to compel a state to adhere to the rules of international law.

Unlike in the past where military warfare means were regarded as instruments of coercing actors to sustain behaviour that was in line with international law, ever since WW1, sanctions have been viewed as the alternative liberal approach to war.

Article 41 of the United Nations (UN) Charter stipulates that the Security Council (SC) may call upon member states to apply measures not involving the use of armed force in order to maintain or restore international peace and security (Charter of the United Nations). Sanctions are coercive diplomatic measures that are used by states and non state actors in international law to compel a state to change a certain behaviour or policy that violates the principles of international law. The post Cold era witnessed the use of sanctions against states rising at an exponential rate. This is tied to the fact that their growing popularity has avoided a World War from occurring as states now employ diplomatic coercive methods to confront matters of national interest and those threatening international peace and security.

Sanctions have been used to address a wide spectre of issues ranging from terrorism, nuclear proliferation of weapons, human rights violations and democracy only to mention but a few. International law has been the basis of the use of sanctions. Chingono et al. (2013: p. 307) purported that the objectives of sanctions included deterring a target from engaging in unlawful behaviour, compelling an offending state to dispose of or cease behaviour that the sanctioner considered wrongful, changing the target state's behaviour by subverting the incumbent wrong-doers, playing a punitive role or expressing a policy position symbolically to one's own public or to other states in the international system.

The efficacy of sanctions remains a contested issue in the international fora, with increasing protests for the careful designing and monitoring of sanctions in a bid to sustain the foundations of international law. Sanctions may aim at particular items like movement of persons, bar investments, or freeze international financial assets. Much has been written about sanctions and international law in various sanction regimes in the global arena such as those of Iran and Iraq but the case of Zimbabwe seems to have been left out. Henceforth, it is the central interest of this study to analyse the effectiveness of sanctions as a law enforcement tool in international law, the case of Zimbabwe from 2001 to 2013.

[...]

It is imperative to analyse the extent to which travel restrictions were effective in changing the behaviour of the targeted. Without doubt, the travel ban was a major impediment to the targeted as they could no longer go to the destinations of their choices unlike the period prior the imposition of sanctions. The denial of visas was a key inconvenience to those who had personal and business endeavours in the countries which they been denied entry into. In spite of these claims, the travel bans were not clearly defined resulting in the their failure to exert so much needed pressure to compel the behaviour of the targeted ZANU PF elite.

Smith-Hohn (2010: p. 4) emphasises that underscoring this dilemma is the fact that the travel restrictions apply only to certain countries and allow travel exemptions for participation in meetings coordinated by international organisations. Targeted individuals can therefore easily find ways to circumvent the ban—either by travelling to (and shopping in) countries that have not imposed such restrictions, or by attending international conferences or humanitarian events while at the same time pursuing their private interests in whichever countries they visit (ibid). The lack of lucidity on the limitations of the travel ban and the inherent loopholes enabled individuals to outwit the ban thereby culminating a negative effect on the efficacy of the travel restriction. Despite the restriction, President Mugabe and other government officials were still able to attend various international summits thereby exposing the lack of consistency of the travel restrictions.

[…]

Pursuing this further is how the asset freezes managed to compel the behaviour of the targeted individuals. Portela in (ICG, 2012: p. 5) argues that freezes on assets were announced months before they were implemented, affording ample opportunity to move money and valuables. This leaves one to reach to the point that asset freezes were inconsistent, allowing the targeted to shift their treasures hence being ineffective. By August 2005 information from the EU was that assets worth €825,000 had been seized from the government by EU.

[…]

The arms embargoes were undermined by a lack of an international comprehensive arms embargo. Sims et al. (2010: p. 11) observed that despite embargoes placed by some in the West, Zimbabwe's defence ministry remained inextricably linked to arms manufacturers within Europe and the US. An International Peace Information Service Report identified weapons and weapons part transfers occurring within Montenegro (not within the EU) and the US (ibid). Illegal arms trafficking flourished through porous borders between Zimbabwe and its neighbouring countries. Johnson-Thomas & Danssaert (2009) assert that in December 2008 the United Nations Security Council's Group of Experts on the DRC reported several ammunition deliveries of approximately 53 tons of ammunition to the regime of Zimbabwe. On many occasions Zimbabwe received arms from China thereby busting the arms embargo. The lack of an internationally comprehensive arms embargo resulted in the failure of the arms embargo to achieve its objectives.

[…]

Equally important in this manner is how globalisation has rendered sanctions ineffective in the Zimbabwean scenario. This is because globalisation has made it impossible for the sanctions to work as they have given Zimbabwe with alternative trading partners. Globalisation and sanctions are two parallel mechanisms in which the former seeks to unite states and bringing them into a one world village whilst the latter seeks to isolate states. It is paramount to note that the imposed sanctions were imposed at a point in time when globalisation was at its zenith, connecting states by the erasing of borders and through fast communication and transport. Zimbabwe managed to thwart the travel bans, trade embargos and arms embargo. This is also explained by the phenomenon of interdependence which denotes that no state is an island hence states are always in need of each other for trade and regional and international cooperation.

[...]

Sanctions were meant to seize the corruption engineered by the ZANU PF officials, nonetheless, sanctions did not auger well for harnessing corrupt ZANU PF activities. Of notable importance is the controversy surrounding the Chiadzwa diamonds. Sims et al. (2010: p. 15) maintains that shortly after the discovery of diamonds in Chiadzwa, the military intervened to take control of the fields while subjecting artisanal miners and area residents to egregious human rights abuses. As a result, Zimbabwe was suspended from importing and exporting diamonds however, Mugabe and Minister of Mines Obert Mpofu threatened to sell the diamonds outside of the Kimberley Process Certification Scheme. Despite this restriction, the ZANU PF elite continued to benefit from the diamond field at the expense of the people. The diamond fields were estimated to be worth 1 billion to 1.7 billion. Coltart (2013) denotes that sanctions and restrictive measures have been used to cover up massive corruption in the diamond sector particularly the Chiadzwa diamonds. He further argued that in the cabinet whenever they tried to investigate diamond receipts these efforts were always met with the excuse that there was need for secrecy because of sanctions, that if there was a truly transparent process that there would be used by hostile western governments to stop the export of diamonds from Zimbabwe and in so doing have a dramatic effect negative effect on the gross domestic product and revenue flows to the treasury (ibid). One can contend that the secrecy was only meant to benefit the government officials and help them loot more diamonds without checks and balances.

[…]

Critics have criticised the sanctions against Zimbabwe as their negative effects were largely felt by the innocent civilians despite them being targeted against few individuals. Mbanje & Mahuku (2011: p. 4) reiterate that the late 20st Century saw Zimbabwe being dubbed the "Bread basket" of the Southern African region due to its huge agricultural production which resulted in its exportation of surplus grain to its fellow member states of the SADCC (now SADC). From 2000 up to 2009, Zimbabwe's food production declined heavily due to lack of funding to the recently resettled black farmers by the EU as well as ceaseless droughts experienced in the entire Southern African region (ibid). The failure to access funds from the IFI affected Zimbabwe's food security. This is due to the fact that the accomplishments of any land reform programme lies solely on the support new farmers are given in the form of sufficient agricultural inputs. Subsequently the country faced immense food shortages. Basic commodities such as maize, cooking oil, salt, sugar became scarce. The ordinary citizens suffered from starvation. This is in clear violation of international law. This is confirmed by the UN General Assembly in December 1997 voted that starvation of civilians is unlawful. Moreover, the International Conference on Nutrition, World Declaration on Nutrition, Food and Agriculture Organization/World Health Organization in 1992 declared: "We recognize that access to nutritionally adequate and safe food is a right of each individual. We affirm that food must not be used as a tool of political pressure (ibid)".

[…]

Conclusion and Recommendations

While there seems to be a disparity on the nature of sanctions between the sanctioners and the MDC on one hand and ZANU PF on the other hand, the fact that sanctions have a direct effect on the economy and the civilians deems them untargeted sanctions. In a country like Zimbabwe where most of the businesses that sustain the nation are owned by the government officials, the targeted sanctions are most likely to have an impact on the ordinary citizen. It could be that the impact of sanctions on the ordinary citizens was by accident but this inherently made the sanctions ineffective. The research has also revealed that it is certain that there exists a breach of peace due to the lack of democratic norms and violations of human rights perpetrated by the Mugabe regime, despite the likeable double standards of the sanctioners. The validity of the legality of sanctions is justified therefore.

The research has demonstrated that sanctions are not an effective law enforcement tool of international law. The targeted individuals' behaviour deemed impossible to compel. This was due to the incomprehensive nature of sanctions imposed on the targeted. The fact that the West was for the sanctions and the East against sanctions made the travel banned and arms embargoes useless. The research has clarified the reality that the sanctioned targets can always find ways to circumvent the restrictions by connecting with friendly nations. Moreover, globalisation has rendered the isolation of Zimbabwe unfeasible due to the interconnectedness of states and the principle of interdependence which lead to the continuing of trade relations of Zimbabwe and other states. The international sympathy received by the targeted from the international for a contributed to the failure of sanctions to compel the targeted's behaviour.

The sanctions did succeed in applying pressure to the targets; this was witnessed by the formation of the GNU and the inherent drafting of the constitution. Despite the fact that the Mugabe regime had vowed not to negotiate with opposition parties, because of the pressure of sanctions, the regime succumbed to it, making it clear that sanctions were effective in exerting pressure on the targeted. The formulation of the constitution questions also the efficacy of sanctions in the compelling the behaviour of the targets. Moreover, electoral fraud, intimidation and political violence, denial of freedom of expression and association remained unchanged throughout the period under study with exception of a few occasions after the formation of the GNU. Nonetheless, sanctions were used as a scapegoat for ZANU PF's blunders in the past that led to an economic crisis, failure to meet GPA obligations and corrupt activities particularly in the Chiadzwa diamond fields. Sanctions were ineffective in that they did not meet up the desired objectives of the sanctioners. While the underlying principle for the targeted sanctions against ZANU PF was to coerce it to reform, the sanctions realised the contradictory, owing to the impression it gave that ZANU PF was hardening its stance. Moreover, sanctions hurt the innocent civilians harshly. Using sanctions as a law enforcement tool is thus not feasible as it ends up violating the fundamentals of international law, in particular International Human Rights Law.

The predicament does not lie in the imposition of sanctions but in the effects they cause. The effectiveness of sanctions should be improved, by reducing the negative effects of sanctions. This paper concludes that sanctions can harden the targets and at the same time affect negatively the untargeted mostly and thus can be an ineffective enforcement tool for international law.

This study recommends that the government of Zimbabwe adopts democratic norms and principles, diverge from human rights abuses and corruption. It is no doubt that the incompetence of the government of Zimbabwe plays a part in bringing down the economy of Zimbabwe. It is blind to blame the sanctions entirely for Zimbabwe's crisis. To the sanctioners, the study recommends the lifting of sanctions as they have proved to be unnecessary as they hurt the innocent and on the other hand tighten the grip of ZANU PF.

The Symbolic Function of Failed Sanctions

Marcus Boomen

In the following excerpted viewpoint, Marcus Boomen argues the importance of sanctions, despite failure or success. He states that imposed sanctions rarely succeed in changing unethical behavior, and have a humanitarian cost. However, he recognizes that sanctions have the ability to change social interactions and the standard of ethics around the world. Boomen is a research associate at the Seven Pillars Institute for Global Finance and Ethics, an independent nonprofit, non-partisan think tank for research, education, and promotion of financial ethics.

As you read, consider the following questions:

1. Since World War I, what is the success rate of economic sanctions?
2. What are some of the ethical consequences of sanctions?
3. What is the constructivist theory?

E conomic sanctions are an important feature of the modern economic, political and social landscape, lauded as the humanitarian alternative to war, with over 500 cases of sanctions being implemented in the 1990's alone. They are implemented with the stated intention of altering a targeted state's behaviour, to elicit conformity with international ethical norms. An analysis

"The Effectiveness and Ethics of Economic Sanction," by Marcus Boomen, Seven Pillar Institute, July 16, 2014. Reprinted by permission.

of the effectiveness and ethics of economic sanctions reveals they have been a resounding failure. The only focus of academic debate remaining is centred on exactly how ineffective economic sanctions are.

Data and theory demonstrate their clear failure as a means of changing behaviour. Furthermore economic sanctions are not free of ethical cost. They impact innocent civilians and, at worst, can kill more people than the wars they are purported to supplant. Therefore the question must then be asked, why are sanctions still implemented so frequently? The answer: economic sanctions serve a symbolic function. They signal to the target, and the world, what is and is not acceptable ethical behaviour. This is an important act when examined through the ethical lens of constructivist theory. This is a political theory that argues many of our beliefs, behaviours and institutions are consequences of social interaction. Their structures can be and are actively changed, as opposed to the inevitable consequences of nature or necessity. Through this frame work the symbolic function of sanctions is important for it helps construct new ethical norms of belief and behaviour by signalling that acts such as sponsoring terrorism are unacceptable in the world today. The symbolic function serves as an important lesson for people and institutions alike: even when acting ethically seems to have little immediate or evident impact, it is still important to continue. Ethical acts and symbols have the capacity to shape normative practices and beliefs over time.

[…]

Inefficacy in Practice

The track record of success for economic sanctions is not good. They appear to be relatively ineffective at altering a state's behaviour. Not a single study argues sanctions are generally effective.[14] Empirical analysis of the success of economic sanctions by Morgan, Bapat, Krystev (MBK) since WW1 reveals that, at best, they have been successful 34% of the time.[15] At worst, a study by Pape found that only 4% of sanctions succeeded in gaining concessions from the sanctioned state.[16] The discrepancy between these results are attributed to the fact that the MBK dataset includes more cases of minor sanctions, compared to Pape's sample, as well as instances where sanctions were threatened, but not imposed.[17] Among these minor cases, many are trade disputes amongst allies or normally friendly nations who are not at odds over contentious ethical or humanitarian issues. The relative success of economic sanctions should be taken as leaning towards the 5% success rate put forward by Pape. His dataset focuses to a greater extent on the major cases where sanctions were implemented to change unethical behaviour such as genocide, ethnic violence or weapons of mass destruction (WMD) development. Results of UN sanctions in which 98% of sanctions against authoritarian states have failed, corroborate the low success rate against unethical behaviour.[18]

A further contributing factor to the ineffectiveness of economic sanctions appears to be the duration of the action. The longer sanctions are imposed, the less chance they have of succeeding.[19] This result appears to be in direct contradiction with the predictions of the original theory of how sanctions should work. Presumably, operating under a simple utilitarian calculus, the longer sanctions are in place, the greater the negative utility. The greater the likelihood costs out weigh benefits, the more likely is the target to concede. Accounts of why long duration sanctions do not work argue that in circumstances where sanctions are effective they work quickly. Otherwise, the target adapts to the new situation. The result is a situation where the sanctioning state is reluctant to suspend its sanctions, and admit failure.[20] Thus, extending the duration of demonstrably futile sanctions.

Sanctions executed multilaterally, such as those imposed by the UN, are often less effective,[21] a further counterintuitive result. Common sense suggests the more states involved, the higher the cost to the sanctioned state and the less options it has for trade, and the more likely the sanctions will succeed. However, this is often not true for two reasons. Firstly, states may have different levels of commitment to the sanctions. Some may not be willing to stringently enforce them along their borders or through the institutions. This mitigates the potency of sanctions by making them appear half-hearted and creating gaps through which sanctions are circumvented.[22] When many actors are involved, some are incapable of enforcing sanctions due to domestic issues, weak state control, or a lack of resources. This was how Rhodesia's GDP actually rose while it was sanctioned, as its neighbours and their borders provided little resistance to sanction busters.[23] The chances of multilateral sanctions succeeding is minimal unless a major power is resolutely committed to enforcing them, and, even then, sanctions are still unlikely to result in the target changing its negative behaviour.[24]

Ethical Quandaries

Not only is the effectiveness of economic sanctions dubious but they may also bear serious consequences of ethical significance. The prevalent use of sanctions in the last 20 years is in no small measure due to the growth of humanitarianism, as economic pressure is seen as a more acceptable, non-violent alternative to war.[25] The use of sanctions as a more ethical form of coercion is important in many situations because it increases the legitimacy of the sanctioning state and its cause. This was the hope. However economic sanctions come with cost to innocents and civilians.

Comprehensive sanctions can create considerable suffering amongst the populace of the targeted country. A typical example is the sanctions policy imposed on Iraq (1990-2003). The total embargo on Iraq affected the population of 31 million, raising the price of basic commodities by as much as 1000% a year from 1990-95.[26] The embargo crippled infrastructure. Its maintenance could not be financed, and replacement parts could not be obtained.[27] Unemployment became a major problem with figures just prior to the 2003 invasion at 23%.[28] The worst effect of the sanctions was the malnutrition caused by poverty and import restrictions, estimated to have killed 100,000-200,000 children below the age of 5 from 1991-1998.[29] This number alone is higher than the total fatalities of the gulf war, or the estimated 120,000 civilians killed in the war and occupation from 2003-2012.[30]

These sanctions were intended to undermine Saddam Hussein's power but they only strengthened his control.[31] This contradictory result arose from the state becoming the only source of goods or income. The government controlled all food distribution, the vast majority of employment opportunities, and the extraction of resources from both the land and the Iraqi people.[32] The powerful of Iraq were able to maintain their quality of life and increase their control, as the great burden of sanctions fell on minorities, the poor and the weak.[33] Evidently, comprehensive sanctions are not a clear moral alternative to war and their use has ceased. Sanctioning states can not claim to be acting morally while inflicting so much devastation on civilians.

The crisis in Iraq, coupled with those of Yugoslavia and Haiti, resulted in a, "new norm against comprehensive sanctions to become part of the shared understanding among states."[34] Today, smart sanctions are championed as the tool of choice for states wanting moral legitimacy for their cause as there is a common view the humanitarian issue associated with comprehensive sanctions has been solved.[35] It is true the impact of smart sanctions is significantly less than that of comprehensive sanctions, but they are not without costs either.

One type of targeted sanction is an aviation ban which targets a nation's airline industry and stops all companies working with or supplying them.[36] This sanction can have two serious impacts on civilians. Firstly, it restricts or stops transportation of items including agriculture, health care and trade. In countries with poor infrastructure, that puts people at risk, as vaccine shipments, medical evacuations and food supplies are disrupted.[37] Even worse, if people decide to fly they are at great risk as maintenance of aircraft within the state cannot be conducted without replacement parts. This has resulted in 700 deaths from 13 air crashes since 2005 in Iran due to its old fleet, poor maintenance and high costs which stem from the sanctions on its airline industry.[38] Air travel was critical in states such as Libya, Angola and Afghanistan and therefore, these measures designed to stop the rich and powerful from flying put innocents at risk.[39]

Financial sanctions can also be ethically problematic when sanctioning states blacklist banking and financial institutions within a target state. These blacklists ban any banking and financial institution from dealing with the target and so freezes assets as a means of restricting the wealth of the rich.[40] Yet again, this has a great negative impact on much of the population, as many average citizens have savings in national banks which they cannot get back. Nor can the ordinary citizen readily access financial measures such as loans or business transactions as such services become heavily impeded.[41] Punitive measures are taken against anyone who is seen to contravene these blacklists, which results in an issue known as the, "MacDonald's Problem."[42] For example, if all US citizens and companies cannot do business with al-Qaeda, does that mean selling a cheese burger to anyone suspected of association with al-Qaeda is breaking the law? If so, what possible measures can MacDonald's create to monitor its transactions, knowing that it can be heavily penalised for a transgression? This problem has resulted in many companies and individuals being punished and even having their assets frozen for breaching sanctions specifically targeted against terrorist groups.

Smart sanctions may seem a vast improvement on comprehensive sanctions in terms of their reduced impact on innocent civilians, yet they appear to be even more ineffective at changing a target's behaviour. Their utility remains in doubt.

The Constructivist Lens

If both comprehensive and smart sanctions are ineffective and can cause great harm to civilians, then why are they still used so readily by many states? A possible answer is sanctions serve a symbolic purpose. When faced with a crisis or immoral behaviour that is not serious enough to constitute a cause for war, politicians must still take action. Even an ineffective action is perceived at least as acknowledging to the public the sanctioned state is engaging in reprehensible behaviour.[43] Secondly, the imposition of sanctions also is a signal to other governments the sanctioning state disproves of a given act or state of affairs and will not let them pass unopposed.[44] These reasons for action may seem relatively trivial, but this view underestimates the impact such signals have at home and abroad in informing and shaping moral norms of behaviour and belief. This is the manner in which sanctions were effective against Rhodesia and South Africa. In terms of changing government behaviour, these two instances of economic sanctions were failures. The actual economic impact was negligible, as the rise in Rhodesian GDP demonstrates.[45] In both cases, they created a 'rally around the flag' effect in the white populations, which strengthened support for the governments. However, sanctions signalled to everyone the level of racism inherent in Apartheid was immoral and unacceptable. They also showed the black community that many in the world supported its cause.[46]

The idea of measuring the success of economic sanctions in terms of ethics, as symbols to shape normative beliefs and behaviour, is a critical aspect of what is known as constructivist theory. This theory views the world of politics, society and morality as mainly consisting of structures created through human interaction, perception and belief, rather than as a product of inevitable or objective laws of nature.[47] The differences in the way we experience the world shape our beliefs about that world; about what is possible, what is moral, and what is normal. Social facts, such as the acceptability of racism, only exist through social agreement and practice.[48] The best example of this is money. The notes and coins in and of themselves are just paper and metal of little use compared to many goods and services.[49] Without shared agreement and practices, without the belief in money, it is worthless. Over time social facts integrate themselves into our experience to the point they appear to us as eternal, objective reality. This is not to say all things are social constructions and liable to change. There are objective facts, such as humans need to eat and breathe to survive, which are true irrespective of our beliefs about them. However, so much is social construction that much of the perceived world can be changed by changing social norms of practice and belief, even at a global level.

This ability to change our world through social interaction underlines the importance of sanctions as symbols. These symbolic acts have the capacity to change our perceptions of what defines acceptable and unacceptable ethical behaviour in much the same way as symbolic historical acts of protest, such as those of Rosa Parks or the Boston Tea Party. Even if the act of imposing a sanction fails to achieve its immediate ends, the act is an indelible statement highlighting those values we believe to be right or wrong.

Conclusion

Economic sanctions are a tool of a state's foreign policy that have been used frequently for the last 20 years since the fall of communism, and championed as the humane alternative to war. Despite their prevalent use they have conclusively failed in their stated purpose. Sanctions almost never succeed in stopping the unethical behaviour of target states, particularly when enacted over long periods of time or through multilateral actions. Sanctions are not cost-free from an ethical perspective. Comprehensive sanctions especially cause great pain and suffering to the innocent and weak within the sanctioned state's population, as seen with the humanitarian disaster that was Iraq. Smart sanctions have mitigated the worst impacts on civilians but still carry costs that may be difficult to justify when weighed against their comparatively miserable efficacy. The only way economic sanctions make sense is if we view the power of sanctions as symbols in the constructivist light rather than their bare political form. Then, arguably, there is a place for sanctions as a means to shape international ethical norms for the better.

Endnotes
[14] Eriksson "Targeting Peace" (2013), p.280

[15] Morgan, Bapat, Krustev. "The Threat and Imposition of Economic Sanctions, 1971—2000*." (2009), p. 98

[16] Pape, Robert "Why Economic Sanctions Still Do Not Work" International Security 23, no.1 (1998), p. 66

[17] Morgan, Bapat, Krustev. "The Threat and Imposition of Economic Sanctions, 1971—2000*." (2009), p. 98

[18]Eriksson "Targeting Peace" (2013), p.282

[19]Dashti-Gibson, Jaleh, Patricia Davis, and Benjamin Radcliff. "On the determinants of the success of economic sanctions: An empirical analysis." American Journal of Political Science (1997), p.610

[20] Ibd, p.610

[21]Allen, Susan Hannah. "The determinants of economic sanctions success and failure." International Interactions 31, no. 2 (2005), p.132

[22]Drezner, Daniel W. "Bargaining, enforcement, and multilateral sanctions: when is cooperation counterproductive?" International Organization 54, no. 01 (2000), p.97

[23] Hermele, Kenneth, Oden, Bertil "Sanction Dilemmas: Some Implications of Economic Sanctions Against South Africa" (Nordic Africa Institute, 1988), p.17

[24]Drezner "Bargaining, enforcement, and multilateral sanctions" (2000), p.75

[25] Weiss "Sanctions as a foreign policy tool" (1999), p.500

[26] Eriksson "Targeting Peace" (2013), p.282

[27] Bufacchi, Vittorio "Rethinking Violence" (Routledge, 2013), p.68

[28] CIA "Iraq Economic Data (1989-2003)" https://www.cia.gov/library/reports/general-reports-1/iraq_wmd_2004/chap2_annxD.htmlas of 01/20/2014

[29]Drezner, "Sanctions sometimes smart" (2011), p. 97

[30] Iraq Body Count http://www.iraqbodycount.org/as of 01/21/2014

[31] Weiss "Sanctions as a foreign policy tool" (1999), p.501

[32] Eriksson "Targeting Peace" (2013), p.282

[33]Drezner, "Sanctions sometimes smart" (2011), p.99

[34] Solingen "Sanctions, Statecraft, and Nuclear Proliferation" (2012), p.159

[35] Eriksson "Targeting Peace" (2013), p.288

[36] Brzoska, Michael "Design and implementation of arms embargoes and travel and aviation related sanctions, result of the 'Bonn-Berlin Process' " (BICC, 2007), p. 71

[37]Gordon, Joy. "Smart Sanctions Revisited." Ethics & International Affairs 25, no. 03 (2011), p.325

[38] *The Economist* "Iranian Sanctions, Winging it"http://www.economist.com/blogs/gulliver/2013/07/iranian-sanctionsas of 20/01/2014

[39]Gordon "Smart Sanctions Revisited." (2011), p.326

[40] Eriksson "Targeting Peace" (2013), p. 288

[41] Fitzgerald, Peter "Compliance Issues Associated with Targeted Economic Sanctions," in House of

Lords, Select Committee on Economic Affairs, 2nd Report of Session 2006-07, The Impact of

Economic Sanctions, Vol. II: Evidence, p.150

[42]Gordon "Smart Sanctions Revisited." (2011), p.328

[43] Whang, Taehee. "Playing to the Home Crowd? Symbolic Use of Economic Sanctions in the United States1." International Studies Quarterly 55, no. 3 (2011), p.788

[44] Ibd, p. 787

[45] Mack, Andrew, and Asif Khan. "The efficacy of UN sanctions." Security Dialogue 31, no. 3 (2000), p.282

[46] General Accounting Office of the United States of America "Economic Sanctions, Effectiveness as Tools of Foreign Policy" (DIANE Publishing, 1993), p.28

[47] Roberts, Peri "Political Constructivism" Routledge, 2007), p.1

[48] Frueh, Jamie "Political Identity and Social Change: The Remaking of the South African Social Order" (SUNY Press, 2003), p.10

[49] Barkin, Samuel J. "Social Construction and the Logic of Money: Financial Predominance and International Economic Leadership" (SUNY Press, 2003), p.25

Using Economic Sanctions to Prevent Deadly Conflict

Elizabeth S. Rogers

In the following excerpted viewpoint, Elizabeth S. Rogers argues for ways in which sanctions may become a more effective instrument in preventing humanitarian crimes and behavior. She contends that states that impose sanctions must be fully aware of regional conflict and predict their occurrences in targeted states. With this knowledge, sanctions strategies can be specific and perhaps successful. Rogers is a former associate and fellow of the International Security Program at the Belfer Center for Science and International Affairs, Harvard Kennedy School.

As you read, consider the following questions:

1. During the years 1989 to 1992, how many armed conflicts ignited around the world within country borders?
2. According to the author, what four rules should be followed to maximize the effectiveness of sanctions?
3. What are the benefits of freezing assets to prevent deadly conflict?

Outside powers could use economic sanctions to prevent an internal conflict if they could foresee an impending civil war and could pressure one or both of the colliding parties to adopt more peaceful policies. For example, governments could

"Using Economic Sanctions to Prevent Deadly Conflict," by Elizabeth S. Rogers, The President and Fellows of Harvard College, May 1996. Reprinted by permission.

be pressured to adopt reforms that would defuse impending rebellions. Such reforms might include implementing democratic changes, granting autonomy to or sharing power with national minorities, land reform, redistribution of wealth, or refraining from disseminating hate propaganda. The sanctions that pressured South Africa to end apartheid could be considered a successful conflict prevention effort.

Sanctions efforts of this sort are worth attempting because it is far easier to prevent a conflict than to resolve it. If the parties are not yet politically mobilized for war, they will be more tractable.

There are, however, three serious impediments to using economic sanctions for conflict prevention. First, violent internal conflict is hard to predict. It is seldom clear where conflict-prevention measures are needed. Second, the causes and preventives of civil wars can be difficult to distinguish and if they are confused, attempts at preventing can make things worse. For example, Rwanda in the 1990s and Nicaragua in the 1970s are examples of outside pressure contributing to the outbreak of war.59 The successful use of sanctions to prevent conflicts requires good intelligence and a good understanding of the roots of internal conflict in order to avoid costly mistakes. Pressing regimes to respect human rights even at the risk of triggering violence can, of course, sometimes be the best choice. In the Nicaraguan case, the Somoza regime brutally violated human rights, and its removal achieved an important goal.

Third, it is especially difficult to impose sanctions against non-governmental civil parties. Often no clear geographic border separates the opposition from the government, making trade sanctions problematic.[60] Also, these groups are generally not direct recipients of foreign economic aid. Finally, freezing assets is often not an option either because the opposition members are not wealthy enough to have extensive assets in foreign banks, or because secrecy makes it difficult to identify the individuals whose assets should be frozen.[61]

Thus, the prospects for using economic sanctions to prevent internal warfare are mixed. That conflict prevention involves deterrence rather than compellence bodes well for sanctions' success. The greatest difficulty with using sanctions to prevent civil conflict is not with the power of the tool, but the wisdom of its user. There are limits to our ability to recognize when civil war is imminent and to distinguish when reform pressures will prevent war (as in South Africa) and when such pressures will trigger war (as in Rwanda). To use sanctions effectively for conflict prevention, we will need excellent intelligence and a better understanding of the causes of war.

Preventing Interstate Conflict

Most regional violence is internal in nature. The years 1989-1992 saw 82 armed conflicts around the world in which at least 1000 people were killed. Of these, seventy-nine took place within country borders.[62] Nevertheless, regional interstate conflict can pose serious costs and risks to world peace (witness the costs and hazards of the Arab-Israeli conflict). Hence the world's major powers should have an active strategy for its control. How much can economic sanctions contribute to such a strategy?

Sanctions have a fair chance of succeeding when applied to prevent regional interstate wars. Interstate wars can begin in two ways. Either a civil war widens to engulf other states, or war can erupt between two states that suffer no civil conflict. Outside powers can become involved in civil wars in two ways. First, they can intervene in a civil war, as Germany and Italy did in the Spanish civil war, and as the United States did in the Vietnamese civil war. Second, belligerents in the civil war can attack outside powers. Examples include Sandinista attacks on Honduras in the 1970s and Vietnamese communist intrusions into Cambodia in the 1960s and 1970s.

The threat of economic sanctions could help to avert both scenarios. Specifically, an international coalition could avert the first scenario by threatening tough sanctions against any outside powers that intervene, and could avert the second scenario by threatening to sanction either civil belligerent if it attacks surrounding states.

Economic sanctions and the threat of sanctions both seem well-adapted to prevent outside intervention in civil wars. First, success requires the deterrence of a contemplated action, rather than the more difficult task of compelling the reversal of actions already undertaken. Second, it is relatively easy to identify the outside powers who might intervene in a given civil war. Hence the target of the threat (and of the sanction) is clear. As noted above, this is not always true of internal conflict prevention efforts.

It may be more difficult to prevent belligerents from lashing out at neighboring states because the belligerents are highly motivated and therefore less likely to be swayed by economic sanctions or the threat of sanctions. However, even here a sanctioning coalition can be successful if its aid or trade is critical to a belligerent's war effort, or to its post-war rebuilding effort.[63]

Sanctions are likely to be more successful at preventing interstate war than civil conflict for several reasons. Many of the difficulties associated with using sanctions for preventing internal conflict are absent. Determining when and where the risk of war is rising is easier because unlike civil wars, interstate conflicts seldom erupt without warning. It is also easy to identify the parties that must be deterred to prevent an interstate war.[64] With inter-state conflict, the targets of the sanctions (or threats) are nearly always states.[65] Predicting which states are likely to be drawn into the conflict is relatively easy. Neighboring states, former colonial powers, and superpowers are the obvious candidates. Finally, the problem of distinguishing between causes and preventives of conflict is less of a problem.

How Should Economic Sanctions be Applied?

Policy makers should follow four rules to maximize the effectiveness of sanctions. Total and complete sanctions should be imposed. They should be imposed immediately. Gaining the cooperation of key states is necessary. Finally, members of the sanctioning coalition must demonstrate resolve.

First, the full range of economic instruments available should be used. A combination of aid, trade and financial sanctions is markedly more effective than any lesser combination. The total sanctions imposed on Iran (1979), Iraq (1990), Haiti (1991), and Yugoslavia (1992) show that total sanctions achieve results.

Second, total sanctions should be imposed as soon as any decision to impose sanctions is taken. A slow incremental tightening of sanctions is far less effective because it allows the target time to adjust by taking steps—such as stock piling goods and moving money—that would make future sanctions less effective. Slow incremental sanctions may also cause the target to question whether the coalition has the resolve to see the sanctions through to success.[66]

Third, the cooperation of the neighbors, major trading partners of the target, and major aid donors must be secured. Clearly it is desirable to have as many states as possible participate in the sanctions effort. However, the cooperation of these particular states is critical since they have the greatest economic interaction with the target. Gaining their cooperation may not be easy because the neighbors and trading partners are likely to suffer from the imposition of economic sanctions. To encourage cooperation, the UN or the US could provide carrots, such as measures to compensate for the loss of revenue from trade with the target, and sticks such as threats to reduce aid or trade. Carrots and sticks will seldom induce perfect compliance. Even if neighboring governments cooperate, some degree of smuggling is likely. Fortunately, perfect compliance is not required for sanctions' success. The results in Iraq and Haiti demonstrate that a little leakage does not prevent sanctions from devastating the target state's economy.

Fourth, the sanctioning coalition must convince the target that it will keep the sanctions in place until they achieve success. This is especially important because sanctions generally take years to produce results.[67] To create the appearance of endurance, the US must publicly commit itself in a highly visible way to maintaining sanctions until the target complies. Such a commitment from the world's most powerful state dampens target states' hopes of a retreat.[68]

Secondary Sanctions Business

Secondary sanctions apply to non-U.S. persons for wholly non-U.S. conduct that occurs entirely outside U.S. jurisdiction. Compare this to primary sanctions, which prohibit U.S. persons from engaging in specified activities with certain countries, entities, and persons.

Under secondary sanctions, the U.S. government can place the offending non-U.S. person on either the Specially Designated National (SDN) List or on the Foreign Sanctions Evaders (FSE) List. In either case, once listed, U.S. persons are prohibited from doing business with the sanctioned non-U.S. person. Secondary sanctions are a large part of U.S. sanctions against Iran and are becoming a larger part of U.S. sanctions against North Korea.

U.S. persons should ensure that their activities do not facilitate the activities of non-U.S. persons dealing with Iran or North Korea and that they are not dealing with a non-U.S. person on one of the restricted parties lists.

"Secondary Sanctions Can Prove Tricky for Both U.S. and Non-U.S. Companies", by Doreen Edelman, Baker Donelson, July 25, 2016.

Financial Sanctions: Under-studied and Under-used

Financial sanctions have been little used and little studied. Yet, two major types of financial sanctions—freezing assets and political aid conditionality by IFIs—have clear advantages as policy tools. Freezing assets has the advantage of being a precision guided weapon that can zero in on government officials and their supporting elites without causing extensive collateral damage to the largely innocent civilian population. Thus, freezing assets avoids the moral criticism made against economic sanctions, that they unfairly punish the ordinary people of a target state without causing serious suffering to the elites. IFI political aid conditionality also has a built-in advantage in that most of the countries where war is likely to break out are places that badly want assistance from multilateral banks.69 Hence IFIs have large potential leverage.

Given these advantages, why have these sanctions been so little used? In the case of IFI conditionality the answer is relatively simple. IFIs have always seen their mission primarily in economic, not political terms. They chose loan recipients based on economic criteria, not political criteria.[70] This IFI culture is softening as IFIs have since the mid-1980s become more willing to consider environmental issues, poverty, government corruption, and military spending levels in making their decisions.[71] The timing of recent announcements promising aid to Boris Yeltsin's Russia illustrates this changing attitude. But the IFIs apolitical cultural legacy limits their willingness to employ political conditionality widely.

Why have assets been frozen so infrequently? Trade embargoes and bilateral aid cuts have been the economic tools of choice, while assets of target regimes were seldom frozen.[72] One possible explanation lies in the culture of the banking industry. Banking is an unusual industry in that it has virtually no fixed assets. It is an industry based almost solely on trust and relationships. Therefore, bankers are reluctant to take actions that damage their relationships with clients and place future business in jeopardy.[73] Banking industry culture is important because bankers often have large influence on sanctions related policy decisions in the US.

Another possible explanation for the US reluctance to freeze assets is the difficulty in gaining widespread international cooperation. Corrupt and thuggish rulers often spread their money around, placing deposits in many banks in many countries. For example, it was reported in late 1995 that the family of former Mexican President Carlos Salinas had ninety bank accounts in nine countries.[74] This suggests that for asset freezes to have a significant impact, there must be broad international cooperation with the effort. If such cooperation seems unlikely, states may be reluctant to unilaterally freeze assets since this would impose costs on their own banking industry that would not be borne by foreign competitors.

The concern that freezing assets will scare off future depositors may be overblown. First, it is likely that the only investors deterred will be other corrupt and thuggish rulers. Fortunately, there are only a few such individuals, so lost banking profits are small. Second, although the US has frozen assets with increased frequency over the last fifteen years (e.g. Iran, Libya, Panama, and Iraq), no literature has emerged suggesting that the costs to the US banking industry are high. Third, any costs in terms of future deposits lost must be weighed against the large benefits that an asset freeze can achieve. It need not be universal to produce some benefit. Even a unilateral or small scale multilateral effort will reduce the pool of money available to the target, thereby forcing unfrozen accounts to be drawn down. The sanctions against Iraq are an example. Years of sanctions (including an asset freeze), have forced Saddam to exhaust the funds he held in Swiss banks.[75]

Both freezing assets and political aid conditionality have been largely ignored in the sanctions' literature. Sanctions specialists have focused their studies on specific cases such as South Africa, COCOM, and Cuba, rather than specific types of economic sanctions. Since freezing assets has been so infrequent and IFI conditionality is a relatively new option, it is not surprising that neither has received a great deal of attention in the sanctions' literature.[76] These are both clearly important areas for future research.

What are the prospects for using asset freezes and IFI political aid conditionality to prevent deadly conflict? Both of these tools could be very helpful in that effort, and the general trends towards greater use of these instruments makes it more likely that they will be used for this purpose.

Freezing the assets of dictatorial governments and their key supporters could help to ease them from power or induce them to make policy changes that reduce the likelihood of deadly conflict. The recent decisions to freeze assets in Iraq and Haiti are encouraging signs of the willingness of the US and other industrial democracies to use this tool. Also encouraging was the recent decision by the World Court ordering Swiss banks to release some of the assets of former Philippine ruler Ferdinand Marcos to compensate his victims in the Philippines. These decisions suggest that the anti-freezing banker culture is fading or giving way to the policy concerns of the industrial democracies and they raise the possibility of greater future cooperation on asset freezing. By raising the possibility that frozen assets could become forever lost, the court decision could also deter future dictators from taking any steps that might cause their overseas assets to be frozen.

IFIs clearly have an interest in preventing deadly conflict since their investments are lost in the devastation of war and they will be called upon to provide massive financial assistance to rebuild countries when wars end. Thus, assisting in prevention efforts could save them a great deal of money and effort. The recent willingness of the IMF and the World Bank to link high levels of military spending with a lack of economic development indicates a willingness to consider factors related to deadly conflict.[77] However, the experience of the European Bank of Reconstruction and Development (EBRD) sounds a cautionary note. It illustrates the difficulties involved in moving IFIs away from their traditional banking mission towards an active consideration of political conditions in recipient countries.[78]

Conclusions

Economic sanctions have not historically been used for the purpose of preventing deadly conflict. They should be. Conditions for using economic sanctions for this purpose are more auspicious today than in the past and should remain so for the foreseeable future. The Iraq, Haiti, and Yugoslavia cases show that when an international coalition applies immediate and total sanctions, the sanctions can pay policy dividends. The Haitian case shows that even badly designed sanctions, once corrected, can help sender states to achieve their policy goals.

Economic sanctions are more effective than most analysts suggest. Their efficacy is underrated in part because unlike other foreign policy instruments, sanctions have no natural advocate or constituency. Business leaders tend to dislike sanctions because they disrupt international commerce. Most governments have counterparts to the US State Department, CIA, and Defense Department. These bureaucracies are natural advocates for the use of their own tools—diplomacy, covert action, and military force. Economic sanctions have no equivalent champion. As a result, their successes are widely unreported while their failures are exaggerated by those with an interest in either avoiding their use, or in using other instruments. However, economic sanctions are an important policy tool and deserve more attention from both scholars and policy makers.

The main impediment to successfully using economic sanctions to prevent deadly conflict is not the weakness of the instrument. Rather, it lies in the sanctioners' understanding of regional conflict and their inability to act decisively. To use sanctions successfully, sanctioners must gain a better grasp of the roots of regional wars, learn to better predict their occurrence, and become better able to decide on effective solutions. The United States and other sanctioners must also recognize the need to commit publicly to maintaining sanctions for long periods. Finally, sanctioners must formulate a strategy for addressing the economic suffering of domestic interests and neighboring states that are injured by sanctions. These innovations will make economic sanctions an even more effective instrument.

Endnotes

59. Arguing that international mediators and the use of economic leverage contributed to the genocide in Rwanda is Alan J. Kuperman, "The Other Lesson of Rwanda: Mediators Sometimes Do More Damage Than Good," SAIS Review 16, no. 1 (Winter-Spring 1996): 221-240. Pressing regimes to respect human rights even at the risk of triggering violence can, of course, sometimes be the best choice. In the Nicaraguan case, the Somoza regime brutally violated human rights, and its removal achieved an important goal.

60. Pre-war Bosnia with its ethnic intermingling illustrates this problem. UN sanctions against UNITA held territory in Angola demonstrate that this issue does not apply once war is underway.

61. President Clinton's decision to freeze the assets of members of the Colombia-based Cali drug cartel, to threaten sanctions on those states that launder drug money, and to prohibit US corporations from conducting business with members of the cartel or its front companies perhaps indicates a new willingness by the United States to identify and target non-state actors. Alison Mitchell, "U.S. Freezes Assets of Cartel in New Effort Against Drugs," New York Times 23 October 1995, A11.

62. United Nations Development Program, Human Development Report. 1994 (New York: Oxford University Press, 1994), 47, quoted in Weiner, Global Migration Crisis, 17.
63. Sanctions will be more effective if married to threats to assist opponents either economically or militarily.
64. The 1995 U.S. threat to impose economic sanctions on Croatia should it use military force in eastern Slavonia is an example of using sanctions to prevent interstate conflict. Roger Cohen, "U.S. Cooling Ties To Croatia After Winking At Its Buildup," *New York Times* 28 October 1995, Al.
65. The exception would be cases of civil war in which a non-governmental belligerent attacks outward in hopes of widening the conflict.
66. For the opposite argument, that moderate sanctions with the threat of escalation are best, see Ivan Eland, "Economic Sanctions as Tools of Foreign Policy," in *Economic Sanctions*, 29-42.
67. The average duration of sanctions coded as successes by Hufbauer, Schott, and Elliott was 2.9 years. Hufbauer, Schott, and Elliott, Economic Sanctions Reconsidered, 1:101.
68. If the target believes that the sanctions will be short lived, then its willingness to comply with the terms of the sanctions declines greatly.
69. In the 1990s there have been two major causes of war-the breakup of empires and the democratization of multi-ethnic states. All of the states in these categories need development assistance. This argument on the causes of war comes from Stephen Van Evera, "Future of War" seminar presentation, MIT, December 1995.
70. For example, the World Bank's Articles of Agreement state that, "the Bank and its officers shall not interfere in the political affairs of any member, nor shall they be influenced in their decisions by the political character of the member or members concerned." Cited in Wolfgang H. Reinicke, "Cooperative Security and the Political Economy of Nonproliferation," in Global Engagement: Cooperation and Security in the 21st Century ed. Janne E. Nolan (Washington, D.C.: Brookings, 1994), 200.
71. Wolfgang Reinicke notes that the World Bank and IMF now consider these issues to be an integral part of economic development where they were previously considered secondary or incidental. Reinicke, "Can International Financial Institutions Prevent Internal Violence? The Sources of Ethno-National Conflict in Transitional Societies," in Preventing Conflict in the Post-Communist World: Mobilizing International and Regional Organizations Abram and Antonia Handler Chayes, eds. (Washington, D.C.: Brookings, 1996), 291-92.
72. For example, a preliminary count reveals that the U.S. froze assets in less than ten percent of its sanctions efforts between 1914 and 1996. Hufbauer, Schott, and Elliott, Economic Sanctions Reconsidered.
73. A striking illustration of this culture in action is found in Britain's decision to transfer $28,349,440 of Czech gold from London to Berlin in the summer of 1939. Willimson Murray, The Change in the European Balance of Power, 1938-1939: The Path to Ruin (Princeton: Princeton University Press, 1984), 291.
74. Monitor Radio, December 1995.
75. Ibrahim, "Iraq Said to Sell Oil In Secret Plan."
76. This is especially true of freezing assets, a topic that has largely been ignored by political scientists and economists. With rare exceptions, the academic writing on this subject consists of a few highly technical articles in law journals on the mechanics of asset freezes. Two such exceptions, both focusing on the U.S.

freezing of Iran's assets in 1979, are Mahysh Alerassool, Freezing Assets: The USA and the Most Effective Economic Sanction (New York: St. Martins, 1993); and Robert Carswell and Richard J. Davis, "The Economic and Financial Pressures: Freeze and Sanctions," in American Hostages in Iran: The Conduct of a Crisis, Warren Christopher et. al. (New Haven: Yale University Press, 1985), 173-200.

77. Reinicke, "Cooperative Security and the Political Economy of Nonproliferation," 199.

78. EBRD was founded in May 1990 to help the states of Eastern and Central Europe make the transition from command to market economies. Unlike other IFIs, its charter explicitly obligated the bank to lend money only to countries committed to "the principles of multiparty democracy, pluralism and market economics." However, over the last three years the bank has moved steadily away from active political conditionality to become "an operationally apolitical institution wholly focused on financial transactions." Cited in Melanie H. Stein, "Conflict Prevention in Transition Economies: A Role for the European Band for Reconstruction and Development?" In Preventing Conflict in the Post-Communist World, 341, 352.

Periodical and Internet Sources Bibliography

The following articles have been selected to supplement the diverse views presented in this chapter.

Jonathan Marcus, "Analysis: Do Economic Sanctions Work?" BBC News Service, July 26, 2010. http://www.bbc.com/news/world -middle-east-10742109.

Carla Anne Robbins, "Why Economic Sanctions Rarely Work," *Bloomberg Business Week*, May 24, 2013. https://www.bloomberg .com/news/articles/2013-05-23/why-economic-sanctions-rarely -work.

Ian Bremmer, "How U.S. Sanctions Are Working (Or Not) in 5 Countries," *Time*, July 31, 2017. https://www.eurasiagroup .net/live-post/how-us-sanctions-are-working-or-not-in-5 -countries.

Emily Cashen, "The Impact of Economic Sanctions," *World Finance*, April 20, 2017. https://www.worldfinance.com/special-reports /the-impact-of-economic-sanctions.

John Cassidy, "Iran Nuke Deal: Do Economic Sanctions Work After All?" *New Yorker*, November 25, 2013. https://www.newyorker .com/news/john-cassidy/iran-nuke-deal-do-economic-sanctions -work-after-all.

Bryan Early, "Explaining Which International Organizations Can Best Contribute to the Success of Economic Sanctions," Cato Institute, December 1, 2014. https://www.cato-unbound .org/2014/12/01/bryan-early/explaining-which-international -organizations-can-best-contribute-success.

Michael Gorodiloff, "Just How Effective Are Sanctions as a Tool of Foreign Policy?" *Russia Direct*, August 12, 2015. http://www .russia-direct.org/opinion/just-how-effective-are-sanctions-tool -foreign-policy.

Michael Penfold, "Could Economic Sanctions Against Venezuela Backfire?" Wilson Center, September 1, 2017. https://www .wilsoncenter.org/article/could-economic-sanctions-against -venezuela-backfire.

Ralph Peters, "When Sanctions Work—And Why They Fail," *New York Post*, March 24, 2017. https://nypost.com/2017/03/24/when -sanctions-work-and-why-they-fail.

Adam Taylor, "Do Sanctions Work? The Evidence Isn't Compelling," *Washington Post*, August 2, 2017. https://www.washingtonpost.com/news/worldviews/wp/2017/08/02/do-sanctions-work-the-evidence-isnt-compelling/?utm_term=.2b2605bc348b.

CHAPTER 3

Economic Sanctions and Terrorism

Economic Globalization Negatively Affects Transnational Terrorism

Quan Li and Drew Schaub

In the following excerpted viewpoint, Quan Li and Drew Schaub argue the positive and negative influences of globalization of transnational terrorism. Some scholars say that economic openness encourages terrorist activity, while others argue that it fights terrorism. The authors analyzed statistically the effect of economic globalization on terrorist incidents from over 112 countries during 1975 to 1997. Li is Professor of Political Science at Texas A&M University. His research has appeared in over thirty articles in numerous journals and two coauthored books.

As you read, consider the following questions:

1. How does the international trade network help transnational terrorists?
2. According to the study by Krueger and Maleckova, what is the link between poverty and terrorist activities?
3. How can economic globalization help reduce terrorist activity?

D o countries that are more integrated into the global economy also experience more transnational terrorist incidents within

"Economic Globalization and Transnational Terrorism," by Quan li and Drew Schaub, Sage Publications, Inc., April 2004. Reprinted by permission.

their borders? In the months following September 11, 2001, many people questioned the future viability of an open global economy, believing that economic globalization had contributed to the transnational terrorist attacks on the World Trade Center and the Pentagon. Indeed, more than $1.4 billion of goods cross the borders of the North American Free Trade Agreement (NAFTA) countries every day (McDonald 2002). In the last year alone, cargo vessels off-loaded roughly 18 million, 40-foot-long cargo containers at American ports, often in single batches as large as 8,000. Ports and border crossings around the world have similarly experienced an increasing volume of daily shipping and trucking activity. The increasing numbers of trucks and container vessels that facilitate international commerce increase the likelihood of a terrorist successfully smuggling himself or a weapon undetected across a vulnerable border. Financial markets have also experienced a drastic increase in the volume of cross-national transactions. The daily turnover in the foreign exchange market is nearly $2 trillion, exceeding the value of all traded goods and services. The growing number of international financial transactions threatens to overwhelm the enforcement officers who attempt to intercept money meant to sponsor acts of terrorism. Therefore, the risks facing international criminals—including terrorists—who use global networks to facilitate their operations decrease substantially. The global war on terrorism after September 11 has led to tightened security almost around the world, increasing the costs associated with conducting international business.

In contrast, a small number of scholars and policy makers argue that economic openness will result in a reduction in transnational terrorism. Proponents of this view believe that economic globalization promotes economic development, which in turn alters the decision calculus of terrorist groups toward a reduction in terrorist activities. Progress in economic development due to trade and capital flows removes one of the main incentives for people to engage in terrorist activities out of desperation and poverty. Although this argument is relatively new and less well

The UN Security Council Sanctions Strive for Peace

The Security Council can take action to maintain or restore international peace and security under Chapter VII of the United Nations Charter. Sanctions measures, under Article 41, encompass a broad range of enforcement options that do not involve the use of armed force. Since 1966, the Security Council has established 26 sanctions regimes, in Southern Rhodesia, South Africa, the former Yugoslavia, Haiti, Iraq, Angola, Sierra Leone, Somalia, Eritrea, Liberia, DRC, Côte d'Ivoire, Sudan (2), Lebanon, DPRK, Iran, Libya (2), Guinea-Bissau, CAR, Yemen, South Sudan and Mali, as well as against ISIL (Da'esh) and Al-Qaida and the Taliban (2).

Security Council sanctions have taken a number of different forms, in pursuit of a variety of goals. The measures have ranged from comprehensive economic and trade sanctions to more targeted measures such as arms embargoes, travel bans, and financial or commodity restrictions. The Security Council has applied sanctions to support peaceful transitions, deter non-constitutional changes, constrain terrorism, protect human rights and promote non-proliferation.

Sanctions do not operate, succeed or fail in a vacuum. The measures are most effective at maintaining or restoring international peace and security when applied as part of a comprehensive strategy encompassing peacekeeping, peacebuilding and peacemaking. Contrary to the assumption that sanctions are punitive, many regimes are designed to support governments and regions working towards peaceful transition. The Libyan and Guinea Bissau sanctions regimes all exemplify this approach.

"Sanctions," United Nations and the Security Council Affairs Division (DPA).

developed, many policy makers have turned to it for a solution to global terrorism.

[…]

Positive Effect of Economic Globalization on Transnational Terrorism

Many policy makers, journalists, and scholars believe, especially after the terrorist attacks of September 11, that globalization causes an increase in the frequency of transnational terrorism. For example, "the World Trade Center (attack) exposed the dark side of global interconnections: the ease with which the West's enemies and their resources can move around the world" (Is it at risk? 2002). Economic globalization can act as a structural constraint that alters the relative costs between legal and illegal activities and affects the decision calculus of transnational terrorists. More specifically, as globalization increases, the cost of illegal activity declines relative to the cost of legal activity, and the overall level of terrorism increases. This decreased risk results from the expansion of the trade, financial, and production investment networks in the global economy.

Computers, chips, and satellites change significantly the structure of international finance, reducing the risks associated with illegal transnational financial transactions (Strange 1998, 25). The "digitization" of money allows the wide use of credit cards and smart cards, facilitates the instantaneous transfer of funds across borders, and decreases the probability of being caught in transporting and using illegally obtained funds. The integration of the global financial market also leads to an increase in the sheer volume of financial transactions. As the cost of financial transactions decreases, their volume increases significantly. Monetary authorities are less and less able to regulate transactions effectively because those transactions have multiplied so rapidly in number (Strange 1998, 25). The huge volume of financial transactions that occur on a daily basis—more than $1 trillion worth—makes tracing terrorist funds an "extremely difficult task" (Weintraub 2002). Financial globalization therefore limits the area of control that governments have over financial matters, as foreign exchange transactions become practically untraceable (Kobrin 1997). The decreasing effectiveness of governments to monitor financial transactions decreases the risks in the illegal transactions used to sponsor terrorist operations.

Similarly, as the volume of international trade increases, the risk associated with illegal trading also decreases. Trade between the United States, Canada, and Mexico, for example, has more than doubled over the past decade to at least $1.4 billion worth a day. Over the same period, the number of customs agents responsible for discovering contraband or illegally traded goods has remained the same. Statistics concerning maritime shipments demonstrate the phenomenon even more clearly. Of the 18 million cargo containers that arrive by sea each year in the United States, only 2% to 10% of them are searched (McDonald 2002). Other sources claim that the lower estimate is much more accurate (The Trojan box 2002). These figures allow a numerical value to be placed on the level of risk associated with illegal international trade. Obviously, a 2% chance of discovery is much too low to seriously prevent determined terrorist organizations from smuggling weapons of mass destruction across international borders or from conducting profitable illegal trade to finance terrorist operations.

Transnational terrorists also often take advantage of the international trade network to market goods or services in an effort to marshal resources with which to carry out their criminal activities. Terrorist organizations often rely on the international trade network to trade contraband to fund their various operations. The increasingly fluid nature of the global investment and distribution networks makes such trade increasingly less risky and therefore much more likely (Matthew and Shambaugh 1998). For instance, Osama bin Laden's Al Qaeda terrorist network relied on illegal as well as legal international trade to fund its operations (Shahar 2001).

Governments, however, are not well equipped to deal with these changes that facilitate illegal international transactions. For one thing, the number of enforcement officers required to perform proper regulatory and monitory functions is inadequate. "The global financial system provides many more opportunities than it can ever hope to forestall or block . . . law enforcement is playing a game of catch up which it is almost certainly destined to lose" (Strange 1998, 128). Bank examiners and government investigators simply cannot supply the necessary man-hours to effectively monitor the enormous volume of transactions that take place daily (Strange 1998). The failure of governments to provide appropriate levels of enforcement stems not only from the enormous volume of transactions but also from the enormous salary gap for the highly skilled information technology specialists required to fill such positions. As technology continues to drive economic expansion, the government is less competitive financially than the private sector in recruiting the high-tech talent (Naím 2000). The government is limited in its ability to monitor and sanction tech-savvy money-launderers, transnational terrorists, drug traffickers, and other international criminals who rely on the international financial market.

The international banking system also tends toward secrecy, further facilitating the sustained symbiotic relationship between the international banking industry and international criminals (Strange 1998). As banks compete internationally for clients, they must stress their historic pledge to protect the privacy of their customers. Government demands on banks to disclose the illegal banking activities of their customers represent "sticks, without corresponding carrots" (Strange 1998, 131). Banks, threatened with punitive action for failing to disclose any illegal actions by their customers, face a catch-22. If they decide to play above board and deny privacy to the suspicious clientele, they risk losing profit and alienating their entire customer base. Therefore, banks are likely to continue to protect the privacy of their customers and hence implicitly facilitate the continued use of the international financial system by transnational terrorists. An article in *The Wall Street Journal* (Phillips 2002), which discusses the current difficulties of the Bush administration to gain compliance from European banks in aiding the US war on terrorism, suggests that this is indeed the case; international banks are unlikely to disclose the private information of their clientele. Therefore, the relationship between states and banking interests demonstrates yet another way that globalization reduces the costs of operations for transnational terrorist organizations. Matthew and Shambaugh (1998) emphasize the link between the international banking community and transnational terrorist organizations, arguing that only through cooperation with the international banking community can governments hope to "disrupt the transnational web of incentives, opportunities, and capabilities enough to discourage terrorism."

[…]

Negative Effect of Economic Globalization on Transnational Terrorism

Advocates of the negative relationship between economic globalization and terrorism claim that economic globalization removes an important cause of transnational terrorism. The emergence of this argument is quite recent, mostly as an immediate reaction to the terrorist events of September 11. It is not surprising that the argument is not as well developed as those on the positive effect of globalization, nor has it received as much attention from students of transnational terrorism. Economic globalization is argued to reduce transnational terrorist incidents because it facilitates economic development, which in turn removes an incentive to engage in terrorism.

A primary cause of transnational terrorism is underdevelopment and poverty, an argument that recently became popular among but was rarely formalized by policy makers and scholars (see, e.g., Biden 2001; Bush 2002; Johnston 2001; Merritt 2001; Rice 2001; Tyson 2001). Poor economic conditions create "terrorist breeding grounds," where disaffected populations turn to transnational terrorist activities as a solution to their problems. In Marwan Bishara's words, "When people feel so inferior militarily and economically, they adopt asymmetric means—not the usual means—to get what they want" (Johnston 2001). In addition, poverty, underdevelopment, and instability are often associated with those states either willing to provide safe haven for terrorists or unable to successfully expel terrorists from their borders. Poverty and its accompanying instability in Afghanistan created the conditions that allowed the Taliban to gain power, a situation that in turn led to the provision of sanctuary for Al Qaeda and

Osama bin Laden. Consistent with this argument, Bush (2002) claims in a widely cited speech, "We fight against poverty because hope is an answer to terror."

Recently, Krueger and Maleckova (2002) assessed empirically the link between poverty or low education and participation in politically motivated violence and terrorist activities. They show that the occurrences of hate crimes, which resemble terrorism in spirit, are largely unrelated to economic conditions. Then, based on a public opinion poll conducted in the West Bank and Gaza Strip, they show that Palestinians who have higher education or living standards are just as likely to support violence against Israeli targets. Next, they conducted a statistical analysis of participation in Hezbollah in Lebanon and found that education and poverty do not explain whether individuals choose to become martyrs for Hezbollah on suicide missions. Those who have a living standard above the poverty line or a secondary school or higher education are actually more likely to participate in Hezbollah. They also found that Israeli Jews involved in terrorist activities in the early 1980s were well educated and with well-paying jobs. Finally, they show that there is mixed evidence on the effect of real gross domestic product (GDP) growth on the number of terrorist acts each year from 1969 to 1996 in Israel. Krueger and Maleckova conclude that economic conditions and education are largely unrelated to individual participation in and support for terrorism.

Although interesting and innovative, the study by Krueger and Maleckova (2002) needs to be put into perspective. First, most of their cases come from a region that is characterized by historical tension, hatred, and military violence. Their conclusion may not generalize across all countries. Second, the positive relationship between a Hezbollah suicide bomber's education and suicide missions may merely reflect that terrorist leaders use education as a screening device to pick the most competent candidate possible. Without controlling for the job opportunities of the suicide bombers, Krueger and Maleckova are not directly testing their hypothesis. Third, the lack of correlation between poor economic conditions and terrorist activities at the individual level may not be inferred to hold at the country level. Better educated people, living under good conditions in the poor countries, are also better informed about conditions in other rich countries than their poor countrymen and hence are more conscious of the comparison between the rich and their own countries. The sense of relative deprivation can provide a strong incentive for them to engage in terrorist activities as the last resort to change the conditions of their own countries. Their individual behaviors can lead one to observe at the aggregate level more terrorist incidents in the poor countries. Hence, we concur with Krueger and Maleckova that whether economic development is related to transnational terrorism at the country level should be assessed in crosscountry analyses.

For economic globalization to reduce transnational terrorism, globalization has to be able to promote economic development and reduce poverty. Many policy makers have endorsed the positive effect of globalization on development. Canadian Finance Minister Paul Martin (2001) argues that participation in the global economic system greatly enhances a state's economic development. President Bush (2002) also says, "The vast majority of financing for development comes not from aid, but from trade and domestic capital and foreign investment. . . . So, to be serious about fighting poverty, we must be serious about expanding trade." US Federal Reserve Board Chairman Alan Greenspan (1997) also claims that "the extraordinary changes in global finance on balance have been beneficial in facilitating significant improvements in economic structures and living standards throughout the world." Leaders of the seven major industrial democracies assert in the joint communiqué for the 1996 G7 Summit that "economic growth and progress in today's interdependent world is bound up with the process of globalization" (Lyon G7 Summit 1996).

Scholars, however, have relatively more diverse opinions about the effect of economic globalization on development. On one hand, trade was considered to hinder growth in the developing countries in the 1950s. More recently, Rodrik (e.g., 1992, 2001) has raised doubt about the positive effect of trade openness on economic growth for the developing countries. Trade is not sufficient to generate higher growth in these countries, and domestic factors are more important than economic openness. On the other hand, many studies (e.g., Edwards 1993; Frankel and Romer 1999; Stiglitz and Squire 1998) have shown that trade openness does promote economic development. The effects of portfolio and foreign direct investments are also debated in the literature. Although the earlier dependency arguments and the later contagious financial crises in the 1990s led to varying degrees of opposition or reservation concerning capital market integration, there have been equally strong, if not stronger, theoretical arguments and empirical evidence showing that financial and production capital market integration benefits the economic development of countries in general (see, e.g., Graham 2000; Obstfeld 1994; Quinn 1997).

The USA Patriot Act Creates New Duties

Federal Reserve Bank of St. Louis

In the following viewpoint, Federal Reserve Bank of St. Louis discusses the changes enforced by the USA Patriot Act, and how it affects international financial institutions. The changes were made in hopes of creating a greater alliance between the banking industry, regulators, and law enforcement agencies. The Federal Reserve Bank of St. Louis takes great pride in serving "Main Street" audiences and representing their views. The St. Louis Fed is located in the Eighth Federal Reserve District and is a part of the Federal Reserve central bank system that's composed of 12 independent regional Reserve banks and the Board of Governors in Washington, DC.

As you read, consider the following questions:

1. Whom does the USA Patriot Act affect?
2. How is the Patriot Act different from the Bank Secrecy Act?
3. How are correspondent accounts defined by the Patriot Act?

The USA Patriot Act was enacted some six weeks after the tragic terrorist attacks of Sept. 11. The Patriot Act places new or expanded responsibilities on financial institutions, especially those

The First Strike on Global Terror

"We will starve terrorists of funding, turn them against each other, rout them out of their safe hiding places, and bring them to justice."
President George W. Bush
September 24, 2001

The President has directed the first strike on the global terror network today by issuing an Executive Order to starve terrorists of their support funds. The Order expands the Treasury Department's power to target the support structure of terrorist organizations, freeze the U.S. assets and block the U.S. transactions of terrorists and those that support them, and increases our ability to block U.S. assets of, and deny access to U.S. markets to, foreign banks who refuse to cooperate with U.S. authorities to identify and freeze terrorist assets abroad.

Disrupting the Financial Infrastructure of Terrorism

- Targets all individuals and institutions linked to global terrorism.

- Allows the Treasury Department to freeze U.S. assets and block U.S. transactions of any person or institution associated with terrorists or terrorist organizations.

- Names specific individuals and organizations whose assets and transactions are to be blocked.

- Identifies charitable organizations that secretly funnel money to al-Qaeda.

- Provides donors information about charitable groups who fund terrorist organizations.

- States the President's intent to punish those financial institutions at home and abroad that continue to provide resources and/or services to terrorist organizations.

Blocking Terrorist Assets

- The Order prohibits U.S. transactions with those terrorist organizations, leaders, and corporate and charitable fronts listed in the Annex.

- Eleven terrorist organizations are listed in the Order, including organizations that make up the al-Qaeda network.

> - A dozen terrorist leaders are listed, including Osama bin Ladin and his chief lieutenants, three charitable organizations, and one corporate front organization are identified as well.
> - The Order authorizes the Secretary of State and the Secretary of the Treasury to make additional terrorist designations in the coming weeks and months.
>
> *"Fact Sheet on Terrorist Financing Executive Order", by George W. Bush, The White House, September 24, 2001.*

doing business with foreign financial institutions. One purpose of the act is to "prevent, detect, and prosecute international money laundering and the financing of terrorism." The intent is to foster greater cooperation among the banking industry, regulators and law enforcement agencies.

The Patriot Act's definition of financial institutions is broad. It includes securities and commodities dealers and brokers, money transmitters, loan and finance companies, and real estate settlement companies. Some of the act's provisions apply to all financial institutions, while others are more limited in scope. Regardless, all financial institutions should anticipate extensive rule-making. Note: Some provisions will take effect on a given date even if no rules have been issued.

Is This "Know Your Customer" Revisited?

Not necessarily. "Know Your Customer" was far more reaching because it would have required financial institutions to verify their customers' identities and document specific details about their customers' businesses. With the new Patriot Act, the secretary of the Treasury is required only to establish minimum documentation standards. Financial institutions must verify their customers' identities, maintain records and consult government lists of terrorists and terrorist organizations. Those regulations are required to be in place by Oct. 26, 2002.

The Bank Secrecy Act Amendments and General Provisions

The Bank Secrecy Act is the core of US money-laundering efforts. While its anti-laundering requirements are not new for banks, they may be new to other financial institutions.

Establish Programs: Because the Patriot Act mandates that all financial institutions establish anti-money laundering programs, some bank holding companies will need to export their bank secrecy programs to their subsidiaries. These programs must include formal policies and procedures, appointment of a compliance officer, ongoing employee training and independent audits. After consulting with appropriate regulators, the Treasury secretary may set minimum standards for the programs and exempt certain institutions. The section's provisions will become effective this April.

Expanded Protection: If the government receives a voluntary report of a potential violation of the Bank Secrecy Act, financial institutions will be given expanded protection from civil liability to their customers. Additionally, an insured institution is protected, theoretically, if in good faith it discloses facts related to a Bank Secrecy Act violation in a written employment reference requested by another insured financial institution.

Acquisitions and Mergers: One new statutory requirement is that the primary federal regulator, when acting on an application to acquire or merge banks under the Bank Holding Company Act (BHCA) or the Federal Deposit Insurance Act (FDIA), is required to take into consideration a company's effectiveness in combating money laundering.

Increased Penalties: A separate section increases civil and criminal penalties for certain money-laundering violations to at least twice the amount of the transaction, up to a limit of $1 million.

How Will This Affect International Money Laundering?

Effective Dec. 25, 2001, US financial institutions cannot have correspondent accounts for foreign shell banks. The Treasury's implementing rules (published Dec. 28, 2001) define correspondent accounts very broadly to include every imaginable kind of account. The provision applies to securities brokers as well as to depository institutions. The Treasury is particularly interested in industry comments on its definition of these accounts.

Every US financial institution that has correspondent accounts or private banking accounts maintained in the United States for non-US customers must establish special due diligence procedures for opening and maintaining foreign accounts, and for detecting and reporting money laundering.

Minimum standards also are set for enhanced due diligence on the correspondent accounts of foreign banks operating under an offshore banking license or under a license issued by a country designated as "non-cooperative with international money laundering principles." These standards become effective this July, even if the implementing regulations have not been issued.

The Patriot Act also includes a number of other provisions designed to prevent terrorist organizations from using the US financial system without detection or punishment. While many of the financial institutions that the Federal Reserve supervises have robust compliance programs, the recent tragedy illustrates the importance of due diligence.

The Economic Effects of 9/11

Gail Makinen

In following excerpted viewpoint, Gail Makinen evaluates if and how the terrorist acts of 9/11 influenced US economy. He argues that there were small changes to the economy, but that it was a host of events and decisions that influenced those changes. Makinen was a Specialist in Economic Policy at the Congressional Research Service for nearly 20 years. He also served as Economics professor at Wayne State, and is the author of five books and several articles, including "Are Central Bankers Currency Manipulators?" published in the Atlantic Economic Journal.

As you read, consider the following questions:

1. What initial action was taken by the US in the aftermath of the attacks?
2. How has increased security at borders affected the economy?
3. What government programs helped the economic ramifications from 9/11?

The tragedy of September 11, 2001 was so sudden and devastating that it may be difficult at this point in time to write dispassionately and objectively about its effects on the US economy. This retrospective review will attempt such an undertaking. The loss of lives and property on 9/11 was not large enough to have

"The Economic Effects of 9/11: A Retrospective Assessment," by Gail Makinen, Congressional Research Service, September 27, 2002.

had a measurable effect on the productive capacity of the United States even though it had a very significant localized effect on New York City and, to a lesser degree, on the greater Washington, DC area. Thus, for 9/11 to affect the economy it would have had to have affected the price of an important input, such as energy, or had an adverse effect on aggregate demand via such mechanisms as consumer and business confidence, a financial panic or liquidity crisis, or an international run on the dollar.

It was initially thought that aggregate demand was seriously affected, for while the existing data showed that GDP growth was low in the first half of 2001, data published in October showed that GDP had contracted during the 3rd quarter. This led to the claim that "The terrorist attacks pushed a weak economy over the edge into an outright recession." We now know, based on revised data, this is not so. At the time of 9/11 the economy was in its third consecutive quarter of contraction; positive growth resumed in the 4th quarter. This would suggest that any effects from 9/11 on demand were short lived. While this may be true, several events took place before, on, and shortly after 9/11, that made recovery either more rapid than it might have been or made it possible to take place. First, the Federal Reserve had eased credit during the first half of 2001 to stimulate aggregate demand. The economy responds to policy changes with a lag in time. Thus, the public response may have been felt in the 4th quarter giving the appearance that 9/11 had only a limited effect. Second, the Federal Reserve on and immediately after 9/11 took appropriate action to avert a financial panic and liquidity shortage. This was supplemented by support from foreign central banks to shore up the dollar in world markets and limited the contagion of 9/11 from spreading to other national economies. Nevertheless, US trade with other countries, especially Canada, was disrupted. While oil prices spiked briefly, they quickly returned to their pre-9/11 levels.

Thus, it can be argued, timely action contained the short run economic effects of 9/11 on the overall economy. Over the longer run 9/11 will adversely affect US productivity growth because resources are being and will be used to ensure the security of production, distribution, finance, and communication.

[…]

The change in US political, security, and diplomatic relations necessitated by the war on terrorism and Afghan campaign also had economic repercussions. US aid policy took an abrupt turn in favor of providing assistance to Afghanistan and front line states, such as Pakistan and the Central Asian republics. With antiterrorism the overriding aim of US foreign policy, concerns over nuclear tests by Pakistan and India suddenly became less prominent, and most sanctions were lifted to clear the way for economic and/or military assistance to the two nations.

[…]

Actions Undertaken

In the immediate aftermath of the attacks, the central banks of the United States and other nations injected a large amount of liquidity into the world financial system to avoid payment failures and cascading defaults. This liquidity later was withdrawn as the system returned to normal. Other countries also provided some fiscal stimulus to their economies, but most had less leeway to do so than did the United States.

Increased security at borders has impeded international trade flows, but governments are working to ease the bottlenecks. Canada allocated $1.2 billion to enhance border security and improve the infrastructure that supports major border crossings. On September 9, 2002, President Bush and Canadian Prime Minister Jean Chrétien recognized the Free and Secure Trade Program designed to speed pre- screened trucks across the US-Canadian border and facilitate the $1.3 billion in trade each day. The program offers increased integrity in supply chain management by providing expedited clearance processes to those carriers and importers who have enrolled in the US Customs-Trade Partnership Against Terrorism or Canada's Partners in Protection. In December 2002, the crossings in Detroit and five other locations are to have dedicated lanes for trucks whose information is to be instantly verified by computer.

Partly as a result of the poor world economic conditions following 9/11 combined with the need for international cooperation in the war on terrorism, the Bush Administration has taken a somewhat more conciliatory approach toward emergency lending by international financial institutions. After early skepticism of so-called "bailout packages" for countries in financial distress, the US Treasury supported a stand-by credit totaling $2.8 billion from the International Monetary Fund for Uruguay in March, June, and August 2002 and a new $30 billion stand-by credit package for Brazil in August 2002. While the Bush Administration still favors more crisis prevention, shifting more of the "burden of bailouts" to private sector lenders, and limits on official finance, the US Treasury has stated that the United States will support countries that follow the right economic policies (i.e. currently Brazil and Uruguay but no further assistance to Argentina until the Argentine authorities develop a sustainable economic program).[25]

With respect to aid to Afghanistan and Pakistan, in a January 2002 conference on Afghan reconstruction, the United States pledged $297 million in aid, a figure that in FY2002 was being exceeded as the United States provided food, medicine, and other emergency support to that country. Given Pakistan's position as a front line state in the Afghan campaign, the United States lifted economic sanctions on Pakistan and cleared the way for a $1 billion financial package that included $600 million in direct aid, a proposal for $73 million for border security, debt relief, and increased market access for $142 million in Pakistani apparel exports to the United States. In the spring of 2002, as the threat of nuclear war between Pakistan and India arose along the Line of Control dividing Kashmir, it became apparent that the United States continued to have a strong interest in the stability of the region and the prevention of another conflict in Kashmir that could affect US troops and divert attention away from the antiterror campaign. Diplomatic efforts by the United States and other nations temporarily eased tensions, but the threat of war raised security issues that likely will continue to affect US foreign economic policy —particularly sanctions policy. The United States also sent US troops to the Philippines and promised to send military equipment there to help the Philippines in its conflict with the Abu Sayyaf radical Muslim insurgents.

Looking to the Future

In the aftermath of 9/11, it appears that the international economy has currently become a one-locomotive world. Only United States—with some help from China—has had the size and strength to provide the economic stimulus to world economies necessary to help pull them out of the global recession. Japan and Western Europe remained coupled to the US business cycle and have remained dependent on exports for economic recovery rather than relying upon domestic fiscal and monetary policies. The limited recovery in their domestic sectors has been too weak and unsteady to counter the global downturn. For US policymakers, therefore, actions to restore health to the American economy also may determine global economic conditions. In this sense, foreign and domestic economic interests coincide.

US policy options include the usual array of stimulative monetary and fiscal policies. The United States may coordinate monetary and fiscal policies with other nations or use its influence to induce foreign economic policymakers to pursue politically unpopular, but necessary, economic policies or reforms. Foreign economic policymakers also share US interests in strong domestic economies. At times, however, national political, economic, or other considerations arise that hamper the ability of a country to pursue needed economic reforms or policies. This has been the case with Japan, where vested interests have thwarted plans to rid the banks of a large accumulation of nonperforming loans, or with European monetary authorities, who seem overly reluctant to lower interest rates at times because of their fear of rekindling inflationary pressures. While other countries may respond positively to US pressures, such activity also can generate resentment among allies for what can be seen as American interference in domestic affairs.

The effect of terrorism could be significant in raising the costs of international trade because of heightened security measures. While businesses are adjusting, easing these bottlenecks while maintaining security is requiring large capital outlays and more paperwork. Although certain domestic industries would applaud what amounts to increased costs for imports, American exporters also face heightened costs to ship their products to foreign markets. As tariffs and other barriers to trade are being reduced or eliminated through multilateral trade negotiations and free-trade agreements, the possibility exists that non-tariff barriers imposed to assure security, whether warranted or not, may take their place.

The weights given to competing interests of the United States also have shifted because of the antiterror campaign. This has altered the calculus for the use of sanctions to achieve, nonproliferation, human rights, or pro-democracy goals.

Conclusions

Among the major conclusions is that 9/11 is more appropriately viewed as a human tragedy than as an economic calamity. Notwithstanding their dire costs in human life, the direct effects of the attacks were too small and too geographically concentrated to make a significant dent in the nation's economic output. September 11 did not trip a fragile economy into recession. The economy was already in its third consecutive quarter of contraction even though the data showing this were not available until a later time. Moreover, the contraction in the US was coincident with the slowdown in economic growth of the major economies, the first time this had occurred in 25 years. Thus, many of the factors associated with the world slowdown, such as rising unemployment and falling confidence may have been wrongly attributed to 9/11. In the final analysis it may be difficult to separate the effects of the terrorist attacks from the then on-going recession. Individuals may continue to assert that various economic events were caused by 9/11 when, in fact, they were not.

There is, of course, the possibility that, but for the timely and decisive action by the Federal Reserve in concert with other major central banks, the effects of 9/11 on both the US and world economies would have been quite different. In this context it should not be overlooked that markets have powerful mechanisms and incentives to overcome negative shocks. This was typified by the action of individuals in the financial sector to restore their institutions to a normal state of function as quickly as possible. For many observers this has re-validated the wisdom of having a central bank capable of exercising a large amount of discretion.

Although the attacks were unique in American history, several existing government programs and agencies were successfully modified in a short time to cope with the economic ramifications. Successfully modified programs or agencies include FEMA, unemployment programs, monetary policy, and programs to help small businesses, although not to the total satisfaction of the latter. In the case of the financial industry, preparations for Y2K left the industry well prepared to cope with the loss of data and infrastructure in wholly unintended ways. Undoubtedly, much was learned by the affected agencies that will be useful if similar tragedies were to occur in the future. Fiscal policy also responded, but far more slowly than monetary policy initiatives. In the case of the airlines, new legislation was quickly implemented to cope with their special problem. A fiscal response to the threat posed to the insurance industry by terrorism remains in debate. There also remains a largely state issue that has federal consequences in the face of terrorism. Many states operate under balanced budget requirements. Expenditures to remediate the adverse effects of terrorism as well as the destruction of a part of a state's tax base can throw state budgets into deficit and inflict additional hardships on a state's taxpayers as legislatures comply with constitutional requirements to balance budgets. As a result of 9/11, the budget of the state of New York was pushed into deficit forcing some difficult choices on the legislature and, arguably, constraining the ability of the state to address the special needs of New York City. This experience may well lead to future congressional consideration of the appropriate federal role in assisting states, regions, and cities adversely affected by terrorism.

In an important sense 9/11 does mark the end of an era, for it reveals that the United States is vulnerable to attacks on its home soil. One of the major modes of transportation became a vehicle for attacking symbols of America. The attackers were able to board these planes with weapons that were not then deemed to be contraband. But the net effect has been devastating for the passenger airline industry even with the government aid that has been forthcoming. It is now doubtful that the industry will survive in its present state.

In addition to the airline industry, 9/11 had led to the recognition that the nation's food supply may be vulnerable to biological attack, our cities to bio-terrorism, and that American ports could serve as entry points for weapons of mass destruction. This vulnerability has had several effects. First, it has led to a reallocation of national resources toward the production of greater security. This will temporarily affect the growth of productivity adversely, the major factor providing the growth of per capita income. Second, it has and will likely continue to change the business structure of the United States and, to some degree, the structure of other economies as well over the longer run. How Americans spend their leisure time has been changed by 9/11. This may be temporary or longer lasting. This change affects their spending and with it the structure of the industry supplying goods and services for leisure.

Third, the vulnerability of the US to terrorism raises new questions about risk—and the role of government in protecting against risk—in a capitalist economy. The risk posed by terrorism is unlike the risk faced by a typical business firm or household. Unlike a natural disaster, the lack of historical examples makes future risks largely unpredictable. Therefore, businesses cannot fully plan ahead to safeguard against its effects. Unlike a natural disaster, it is a risk addressed by the security that government provides for its citizens. When this security fails or is breached, it can have devastating consequences for selected business firms, geographical areas, and elements in the population. 9/11 had a severe effect on New York City, the airlines industry, and especially the insurance industry. While the latter appears to be able to withstand the claims due to 9/11, it is doubtful if it could withstand several attacks with the consequences of 9/11. Traditionally, there has been an understanding that certain risks, such as war, could not be handled by market mechanisms and required government involvement. The government is now trying to determine the point when terrorism stops being an insurable risk and begins to look more like war. At present, the situation is ambiguous. Private insurers are still willing to insure most firms and projects against terrorism, but some "trophy" projects that make likely targets have not been able to acquire insurance. That is apparently because insurers do not know how to price such risks and insureds may prefer to "self insure" rather than pay very high premiums. This effect would be stronger if firms should think that the federal government is implicitly willing to compensate them in the event of a catastrophe. In this context, the terrorism insurance bills before Congress would seek to make explicit what is now implicit by defining the point past which the government would provide insurance because the private market no longer can. In the absence of such legislation, large or ostentatious projects may continue to have difficulty getting coverage, and as a result fewer such projects may be built in the future. Conversely, legislation could increase the "moral hazard" problem present in the terrorism insurance market: if the federal government steps in to protect against calamitous losses, more trophy projects that make attractive targets will be built. For safety reasons, it can be argued, government may have to assume a role in pricing such that the cost to the private owners of building these types of properties reflects the costs to society.

Endnotes

22 Canada. Department of Foreign Affairs and International Trade. Trade Update. May 2002. Third Annual Report on Canada's State of Trade. Available at: [www.dfait-maeci.gc.ca/eet/state-of-trade-e.asp].

23 Shannon, Elaine. Manning the Bridge. *Time*, September 9, 2002. Pp. 100-104.

24 Organization for Economic Cooperation and Development. OECD Economic Outlook No 71, June 2002. P. 131.

25 Dam, Kenneth W. The Role of the United States in the Global Economy, Remarks by Kenneth W. Dam, Deputy Secretary of the Treasury at the Center for Strategic and International Studies, Washington, D.C., September 11, 2002.

The United States Did Pakistan a Disservice After 9/11

Gary Leupp

In the following viewpoint, written in the years following the start of the War on Terror, Gary Leupp argues that the war on Afghanistan's Taliban regime unleashed a huge problem on the Pakistan state and ultimately did nothing to win the war on terror. The author evaluates every step the US government made towards Pakistan and its neighbor Afghanistan after the events of 9/11 to make his claim. Leupp is Professor of History at Tufts University, and holds a secondary appointment in the Department of Religion.

As you read, consider the following questions:

1. How did the relationship change between the US and Pakistan after 9/11?
2. What is the difference between the Taliban and al-Qaeda?
3. How did the war in Afghanistan affect Pakistan?

Immediately after 9-11 the US government began barking orders to the world, especially to the Muslim world. Perhaps echoing unconsciously the Christian scripture passages Matthew 12:30 and Luke 11:23, it proclaimed, "Either you are with us, or with the terrorists." Remember those terrifying days, of omnipresent institutionalized ritualistic grief, anger and mandated unity, when any questioning was met with official indignation, threats, or

"The U.S. and Pakistan After 9/11," by Gary Leupp, CounterPunch, December 29, 2007. Reprinted by permission.

punishment? When everything was supposed to be so clear? When above all, the national need to attack somebody—some Muslims—was supposed to be obvious, and the attack on Afghanistan in particular framed as common sense?

In Afghanistan, the Taliban was told that Washington would not distinguish between terrorists and the regimes that harbor them. The Taliban was of course one of the fundamentalist Islamist groups emerging from the long US effort (1979-93) to topple the Soviet-supported secular regime. The Taliban in power from 1996 had netted some aid from a Washington deeply interested in Afghan oil pipeline construction, and also received aid and diplomatic support from Pakistan. Pakistan's CIA (the Inter-Service Intelligence or ISI) had helped create the Taliban in order (as Benazir Bhutto later explained) to secure the trade route into Central Asia.

The Taliban, then with US aid suppressing opium poppy production with extraordinary success, and manifesting no special hostility towards Washington, was ordered to hand over 9-11 mastermind Osama bin Ladin. But Pashtun culture (far more than most cultures) mandates that guests receive hospitality and protection, and bin Ladin, a periodic visitor from 1984 and permanent resident since 1996, was no ordinary guest. He had raised or supplied from his personal funds millions of dollars for the anti-Soviet Mujahadeen (which one must always emphasize was supported by him as well as the US), and fought against the secular "socialist" Afghan regime in the name of Islam. Taliban leader Mullah Omar could not simply turn him over to the Americans and maintain any credibility with his own social base. On the other hand, the Taliban did not wish to provoke an invasion. So the Afghans asked for evidence of bin Ladin's complicity in the attacks. Washington treated the request as absurd. The Afghans offered to turn bin Ladin over to an international court of Islamic jurists. The US reiterated its demand that bin Ladin be transferred to American authorities immediately, knowing this was not going to happen and that it would thus have a popularly accepted casus belli.

Meanwhile Pakistan's dictator-president Gen. Pervez Musharraf was told by the US State Department that Pakistan must cut ties to the Taliban. "Be prepared to be bombed. Be prepared to go back to the Stone Age," he was told by US Secretary of State Colin Powell, through his deputy Richard Armitage, if he was unwilling to cooperate in the destruction of Afghanistan's Taliban regime. Musharraf was also ordered to host US troops and prevent anti-US demonstrations in his country. Briefly Pakistan protested that it might be better to preserve diplomatic ties with the Taliban government, in order to influence it to cooperate with the US which (one must repeat) had not hitherto had an unfriendly relationship with the US. But caving into the US diktat, angering ISI officers deeply invested in Taliban support, risking a coup or assassination, Musharraf complied with US demands. He was rewarded with the removal of US sanctions imposed after Pakistan's nuclear tests in 1998, and promises of massive aid as the US prepared to bomb Afghanistan, topple the Talibs and impose following their downfall a government of Afghans willing to work with Washington. This of course turned out to be a government dominated by the Northern Alliance, a collection of non-Pashtuns including Uzbek and Tajik warlords hostile to Pakistan and supported by India and Iran.

The US bombed; the Taliban fell, for the most part retreating to ancestral villages and lying low, monitoring the situation, seeking opportunities for resurgence. Few Americans at the time questioned the Bush administration's ready conflation of the Taliban and al-Qaeda, but the two were and are appreciably different. Al-Qaeda is a mostly Arab but multinational global network of Islamists hostile to the US and its policies towards the Muslim world, growing in strength due to the continuation of those policies; the Taliban is a primarily Pashtun organization reflecting traditional Afghan Muslim fundamentalist values and fiercely opposed to foreign domination. The former is sophisticated, headed by well-educated men; the latter is largely illiterate, headed by clerics learned only in Islamic literature. The former wants to attack multiple targets to foment a generalized confrontation between the West and Islam; the latter wants to mind its own house and maintain Afghan traditions with all their xenophobic, medieval, patriarchal, misogynistic, anti-intellectual appeal.

A mix of Taliban militants and al-Qaeda forces resisted the US invasion; hundreds at least escaped into Pakistan's Federally-Administered Tribal Areas and North-West Frontier Province. Having driven bin Ladin and his followers out of Afghanistan, the US declared a great victory and without skipping a beat moved on to invade and occupy Iraq, which had nothing to do with 9-11. The latter crime inevitably produced outrage globally, but particularly in Muslim countries like Pakistan, where the prestige of bin Ladin, already high in 2001, has soared ever since. (A recent poll showed his approval rating at 46%, compared to Musharraf's 38% and Bush's 9%.)

Preoccupied with establishing an empire, US leaders lost interest in al-Qaeda. Indeed in March 2002 President Bush referring to bin Ladin declared, "I truly am not that concerned about him." As for the al-Qaeda forces in Pakistan (whose very existence close US ally Musharraf denied), they were Pakistan's problem. The US had unleashed a huge problem on the Pakistani state by invading its neighbor, toppling the Afghan government, and forcing al-Qaeda to relocate into Pakistan where sympathetic tribesmen (who have always resisted firm incorporation into the state) offered them safe haven. Pashtuns straddle the boundary of the two countries; Pakistani Pashtuns are largely sympathetic to the Taliban, and now a Pakistani Taliban is growing in strength in the Taliban and elsewhere.

Thus the "good war" in Afghanistan preceding the generally discredited war-based-on-lies in Iraq was in fact a very bad war so far as Pakistan was concerned. It brought Afghanistan a new warlord government, in which opium is again the chief commercial crop, prettified by a "democratic" election and the appointment of a longtime CIA contact, Hamid Karzai as president and de facto mayor or Kabul. It is increasingly challenged by the recrudescent Taliban and new recruits who have regained control of much of the south. Karzai from his weak position keeps offering them peace talks, which they reject, demanding the invaders leave before any negotiations.

For the US the "good war" has meant 474 soldiers dead (116 so far this year); "coalition" dead have increased every year since 2003 and almost as many European troops have died during the last two years as Americans. Support for the Afghan mission has declined in Europe as its relevance to "counter-terrorism" becomes increasingly unclear and its character as an unwinnable counterinsurgency effort becomes more apparent.

The war in Afghanistan saddled Musharraf with a mounting Islamist rebellion in the Swat Valley and elsewhere; grave dissatisfaction within the military at the unprecedented deployment in the frontier provinces (where troops have performed poorly and unenthusiastically against Islamists); and personal unpopularity related both to his ties to the US and to his abuses of power. Adding to his woes, the US military struck targets within his country (without his consent, he claims), and threatened to take further action against Taliban or al-Qaeda forces in Pakistan. Then the Pakistani Chief Justice opposed his bid to run for president again, and needed to be arrested, causing a nasty political crisis. In an embarrassment to Musharraf the Supreme Court ordered the justice's release. In the meantime supporters of former prime ministers Benazir Bhutto and Nawaz Sharif clamored for their return.

The natural thing for a beleaguered strongman to do in such circumstances would be to declare a state of emergency and assume emergency powers. But the US State Department told him no, don't do that, let Bhutto come back, work out some accommodation with her. Let the two of you share power and erect an anti-terrorist united front. So Musharraf hesitated until November, when he did indeed declare a state of emergency, meeting with Washington's public disapproval. The US threatened to cut off some non-military aid if he didn't quickly lift martial law and hold elections in which Bhutto might compete. Musharraf negotiated with Bhutto, trading cancellation of corruption charges against her for his agreement to respect the constitutional provision that disallowed him to be both president and military officer at the same time.

Quite possibly Musharraf was thinking, "These people, who have already done so much to destabilize Pakistan, now want to destabilize it further by forcing me into this." But he did, and Bhutto got killed, maybe by his people (cui bono?), maybe by al-Qaeda, maybe by homegrown Islamists angered by Bhutto's Washington ties, which are even more intimate than Musharraf's.

Maybe Musharraf will now cancel the election. Maybe he will hold it, arranging to win big. Either way, Washington analysts agree his position is weakened by the assassination. Pakistan, more or less stable as of 2001, has in the interval been knocked off balance by US action in the region. Told it must be for or against the US, it was obliged to obey, with grim results.

Unprecedented militant Islamism. Unprecedented support for bin Ladin and al-Qaeda. Unprecedented support for the Taliban. Unprecedented Taliban-like attacks on Buddhist monuments, parts of Pakistan's cultural heritage. The assassination of a popular pro-Western political figure on whom the US State Department had placed its bets. Anti-Musharraf rioting in the wake of the assassination. Dire consequences indeed of Musharraf's alliance.

Is Sudan a Partner in the Fight or a Funder in the War on Terror?

Preeti Bhattacharji

In the following viewpoint, Preeti Bhattacharji analyzes Sudan's designation as a state sponsor of terrorism, and the complexity of the status. Despite Sudan's efforts to coordinate with the international community on terrorism issues, it is still designated as a country repeatedly involved in acts of terror. Bhattacharji is a Vice President of Integrated Capitals at Heron. Prior to joining Heron, she served as an assistant director of the Heilbrunn Center for Graham & Dodd Investing and a research associate for the Council on Foreign Relations.

As you read, consider the following questions:

1. In what ways has Sudan contributed to terrorism?
2. What are the four main sets of US imposed sanctions on Sudan?
3. How has Sudan joined the fight against terrorism?

In August 1993, the US State Department labeled Sudan a "state sponsor of terrorism," alleging it harbored local and international terrorists, including Osama bin Laden. But in recent years, Sudan has signaled a willingness to combat terrorism. In light of this progress, the UN Security Council lifted terrorism-related sanctions against Khartoum in 2001, and in 2007, the US State Department said Sudan had become "a strong partner in

"State Sponsors: Sudan," by Preeti Bhattacharji, Council on Foreign Relations, April 2, 2008. Reprinted by permission.

the War on Terror." But despite Khartoum's new counterterrorism efforts, Sudan remains on the US list of state sponsors because it continues to support Hamas, which the Bush administration considers a terrorist organization. Its relationship with the United States and other Western states also remains troubled because of the humanitarian crisis in Darfur, as well as US allegations that Sudan is assisting the Iraqi insurgency by permitting militants from Sudan and other nations to transit to Iraq.

Does Sudan Sponsor Terrorism?

Despite increasing cooperation by Sudan, the US State Department continues to formally designate it as a "state sponsor of terrorism." The State Department first labeled Sudan a sponsor of terrorism on August 12, 1993. Since then, the United States has accused Sudan of harboring members of al-Qaeda, Hezbollah, Hamas, Palestinian Islamic Jihad, the Abu Nidal Organization, Jamaat al-Islamiyya, and Egyptian Islamic Jihad, each classified as a terrorist organization. In 1996, the UN Security Council placed sanctions on Sudan for harboring suspects wanted for the attempted assassination of President Hosni Mubarak of Egypt. The same year, US investigators linked two Sudanese diplomats to a terrorist cell planning to bomb the UN building in New York. In 1998, al-Qaeda operatives based in Sudan were allegedly involved in the bombings of US embassies in Kenya and Tanzania. Throughout the 1990s, Sudan was also accused of supporting local insurgencies in Uganda, Tunisia, Kenya, Ethiopia, and Eritrea.

But in 1999, Sudan signaled a new willingness to cooperate with counterterrorism measures when it signed the International Convention for the Suppression of Financing of Terrorism. The following year, it ratified the International Convention for the Suppression of Terrorist Bombing, which prompted the UN Security Council to lift its terrorism-related sanctions against Khartoum in 2001.

The United States acknowledged Sudan's new initiatives and, in May 2004, removed it from a list of countries that were "not fully cooperating" in US antiterrorism efforts. By 2007, the US State Department reported that, with the exception of Hamas, the Sudanese government did not openly support the presence of terrorists in Sudan.

But despite Sudan's recent willingness to cooperate, the US State Department continues to designate Sudan a state sponsor of terrorism, meaning a range of economic and military sanctions remain in effect. The chief reason for this designation is because Sudan supports Hamas, which the Bush administration considers a terrorist organization. Sudan has welcomed members of Hamas as legitimate representatives of the Palestinian Authority, though it limits their activities to fundraising. Since 2005, the US State Department has also expressed concern with Sudan's role in the Iraqi insurgency, alleging Sudanese and foreign nationals who transited Sudan have been captured as foreign fighters in Iraq. The Sudanese government says it has worked to disrupt foreign fighters from using Sudan as a logistics base and transit point en route to Iraq.

Is Sudan connected with al-Qaeda?

Sudan does have a historic link with al-Qaeda. When al-Qaeda leader Osama bin Laden left Saudi Arabia in 1991, he moved to Khartoum, where he was protected by a Sudanese regime that had recently imposed Islamic law in Sudan's northern states. While bin Laden was in Sudan, al-Qaeda was involved in a series of terrorist attacks. In 1992, the group bombed two hotels in Yemen, targeting US troops en route to Somalia. In 1995, al-Qaeda took part in an assassination attempt against Egyptian President Mubarak. Additional attacks—such as the 1995 attack in Riyadh and 1996 bombing of the Khobar Towers—may be linked to bin Laden as well, though the evidence is scarce.

Under pressure from the United States and Saudi Arabia, Sudan ejected bin Laden in 1996, and he reestablished his base in Afghanistan. Four years later, the Sudanese government began uprooting al-Qaeda bases in Sudan. In 2005, the US State

Department reported that al-Qaeda elements had not been present in Sudan with the knowledge and consent of the Sudanese government since 2000.

But in 2006, bin Laden's ties with Sudan resurfaced. After the United Nations proposed to send a peacekeeping force to the war-torn region of Darfur, bin Laden released a tape that told his followers to go to Sudan to fight UN troops. Similar messages were repeated the following year by bin Laden's deputy, Ayman al-Zawahiri, and again by bin Laden himself.

The Sudanese government has opposed the presence of non-African UN troops in Darfur, but Sudanese officials have distanced themselves from bin Laden's message. A spokesman for Sudan's foreign ministry responded to bin Laden's message by saying Sudan was "not concerned with any mujahadeen or any crusade or any war with the international community." As of April 2007, there were still no indications that al-Qaeda-affiliated extremists were active in Sudan.

Does Sudan have weapons of mass destruction?

A 2008 report by the nonpartisan Congressional Research Service says Sudan does not have nuclear or biological weapons, nor does it have ballistic or cruise missiles. It has ratified the Nuclear Non-Proliferation Treaty and the Comprehensive Test Ban Treaty, and it has acceded to the Chemical Weapons and Biological Weapons Conventions. But the report also says that despite acceding to the Chemical Weapons Convention in 1999, Sudan has been developing the capability to produce chemical weapons for many years. In order to do so, Sudan has allegedly obtained help from foreign entities, principally in Iraq.

What counterterrorism measures has the United States taken against Sudan?

The designation of Sudan as a state sponsor of terrorism imposes four main sets of US government sanctions:

- A ban on arms-related exports and sales.

- Controls over exports of dual-use items, requiring thirty-day congressional notification for foods or services that could significantly enhance the terrorist-listed country's military capability or ability to support terrorism.

- Prohibitions on economic assistance.

- Imposition of miscellaneous financial and other restrictions, including: requiring the US government to oppose loans by the World Bank and other international financial institutions; lifting diplomatic immunity to allow families of terrorist victims to file civil lawsuits in US courts; denying companies and individuals tax credits for income earned in terrorist-listed countries; denying duty-free treatment of goods exported to the United States; granting the US government the authority to prohibit any US citizen from engaging in a financial transaction with a terrorist-list government without a Treasury Department license; and prohibiting Defense Department contracts above $100,000 with companies controlled by terrorist-list states.

How does Sudan coordinate with the international community on terrorism issues?

In 2000, the United States and Sudan entered into a counterterrorism dialogue, prompting Sudan to close down the Popular Arab and Islamic Conference, which had been functioning as a forum for terrorists. In May 2003, Sudanese authorities raided a suspect terrorist training camp in Kurdufan State, arresting more than a dozen extremists and seizing illegal weapons. Four months later, a Sudanese court convicted a Syrian engineer and two Sudanese nationals of training a group of Saudis, Palestinians, and others to carry out attacks in Iraq, Eritrea, Sudan, and Israel. In August 2004, Sudanese authorities arrested, prosecuted, and convicted Eritreans who had hijacked a Libyan aircraft and forced it to land in Khartoum. Of the twelve major international conventions and protocols against terrorism, Sudan has ratified eleven.

Sudan has also worked with neighboring states to combat terrorism in the region. In 2003, Sudan ratified the African Union's Convention on the Prevention and Combating of Terrorism, and by the end of the year, the Sudanese government had signed additional counterterrorism agreements with Algeria, Yemen, and Ethiopia. In 2004, Sudan cohosted a regional workshop with the UN Office on Drugs and Crime on terrorism and transnational crime. Sudan has also worked to mediate peace between Uganda and the Lord's Resistance Army, a rebel group that has terrorized civilians in an effort to overthrow the Ugandan government.

These efforts have prompted the United States to commend Sudan for its counterterrorism practices. In 2007, the US State Department called Sudan a "strong partner in the War on Terror," and praised Sudan for aggressively pursuing terrorist operations that threatened US interests.

But US-Sudan coordination has been complicated by the ongoing violence in Darfur. In 2006, the US State Department reported that the flow of weapons and personnel between Sudan and most of its neighbors had weakened efforts to stabilize the region. Amidst the violence, many of Sudan's borders remain porous, which allows subversive elements to enter Sudan without alerting government security units. Sudan's continued support for Hamas and its role in contributing fighters for the Iraqi insurgency also hinder coordination efforts with the United States.

Periodical and Internet Sources Bibliography

The following articles have been selected to supplement the diverse views presented in this chapter.

Nikita Blows, "Bitcoin to the Rescue in Economically Unstable Countries," Bitcoin News, January 7, 2018. http://bitcoinist.com /bitcoin-rescue-economically-unstable-countries.

Jessica Durando, "U.S. Adds Osama bin Laden's Son to Global Terrorist List," *USA Today*, January 5, 2017. https://www .usatoday.com/story/news/world/2017/01/05/terrorism -sanctions-osama-bin-laden-son/96197152.

Evan Dyer, "Canada Hasn't Added Any of Its 'Terrorist Travellers' to UN Sanctions List," CBC News, December 20, 2017. http://www .cbc.ca/news/politics/canadians-isis-un-list-interpol-1.4455298.

Peter Flanagan, Corinne A. Goldstein, Peter Lichtenbaum, and Kimberly Strosnider, "Russia and Iran Sanctions: Recent Developments," *National Law Review*, November 9, 2017. https:// www.natlawreview.com/article/russia-and-iran-sanctions-recent -developments.

Global Affairs Canada, "Canadian Sanctions Related to Terrorist Entities, Including Al-Qaida and the Taliban," November 23, 2016. http://www.international.gc.ca/sanctions/countries-pays /terrorists-terroristes.aspx?lang=eng.

Saleha Mohsin, "U.S. Joins with Saudi Arabia, Qatar on New Yemen Sanctions," Bloomberg Politics, October 25, 2017. https://www .bloomberg.com/news/articles/2017-10-25/u-s-imposes-new -yemen-terrorism-sanctions-with-mideast-support.

Karin Strohecker, "Out of U.S. Sanctions, Sudan Tries to Lure Back Investors," Reuters Business News, December 15, 2017. https:// www.reuters.com/article/us-sudan-investment/out-of-u-s -sanctions-sudan-tries-to-lure-back-investors-idUSKBN1E91KL.

Drazen Jorgic, "Pakistan PM Warns U.S. Sanctions Would Be Counter-Productive," Reuters World News, September 11, 2017. https://www.reuters.com/article/us-pakistan-politics-abbasi /pakistan-pm-warns-u-s-sanctions-would-be-counter -productive-idUSKCN1BM1XY.

Nathaniel Popper, Oleg Matsnev, and Ana Vanessa, "Russia and Venezuela's Plan to Sidestep Sanctions: Virtual Currencies," *New*

York Times, January 3, 2018. https://www.nytimes
.com/2018/01/03/technology/russia-venezuela-virtual
-currencies.html.

Samuel Ramani, "China's Approach to North Korea Sanctions,"
Diplomat, January 10, 2018. https://thediplomat.com/2018/01
/chinas-approach-to-north-korea-sanctions.

United Nations Security Council, "Success of Sanctions Regimes in
Defeating Terrorism, Staunching Flow of Weapons Depends on
Resolute, Concerted Action, Security Council Told," Meetings
Coverage and Press Release, May 28, 2014. https://www.un.org
/press/en/2014/sc11416.doc.htm.

GLOBALVIEWPOINTS

CHAPTER 4

The Future of
Economic Sanctions

Learning the Ropes, One United Nations Sanction at a Time

David Cortright, George A. Lopez

In the following excerpted viewpoint, David Cortright and George A. Lopez examine a decade of UN sanction strategies using six generalizations that academic and policy assessments use as a roadmap for viewing sanctions. They attempt to extract lessons learned and identify policy recommendations of future sanctions. Cortright is president of the Fourth Freedom Forum in Goshen, Indiana, and fellow at the Joan B. Kroc Institute for International Peace Studies at the University of Notre Dame. Lopez is faculty fellow at the Joan B. Kroc Institute and professor of government and international studies at the University of Notre Dame.

As you read, consider the following questions:

1. Why doesn't economic success guarantee political success?
2. What did the UN Security Council learn about sanction enforcement?
3. What are sanctions assistance missions?

T he following are essential assumptions that underlie academic and policy assessments of economic sanctions:

1. Economic success does not guarantee political success

Whereas many of the embargoes of previous decades were extremely porous, several of the high-profile cases of the past decade have been very effective in economically isolating the targeted regime. Military interdiction and advanced monitoring and tracking technologies combined to create new possibilities for sealing national borders. This effectiveness was especially evident in the cases of Iraq and Yugoslavia. It was no small irony, then, that the ability actually to isolate an economy did not produce the anticipated political outcomes. The United Nations demonstrated a remarkable ability in a world of economic interdependence to bring some of the targeted economies to a standstill. But to the dismay of decision makers, economic strangulation did not automatically or consistently lead to political compliance, i.e., the decision by a targeted leadership to acquiesce to the dictates of the Security Council regarding issues that generated economic sanctions.

This is not to suggest that sanctions regularly failed to achieve their political objectives. In the UN cases of the past decade sanctions were often successful in exerting bargaining pressure and in several instances contributed significantly to achieving the political purposes defined by the Security Council. But it is important to note that as the sanctions episodes unfolded, this disconnection between substantial economic effect and limited political impact led to frustration and the assumption that sanctions do not work. Some nations began to understand sanctions as instruments of punishment and retribution rather than tools of diplomatic persuasion, which generated cynicism and further criticism of sanctions as a policy instrument.

2. Sanctions can have serious unintended consequences

Compounding the dilemma that economic success did not always produce the desired political compliance, it became clear very early in the decade that the sharpened economic bite of sanctions was wreaking havoc on the wellbeing of vulnerable populations within the targeted countries, especially in Iraq. Traditionally, concerns about the unintended effects of sanctions had focused on the disruption of trade. Article 50 of the UN Charter offered trading partners or neighbouring states of a targeted nation the opportunity to seek compensation to offset the economic losses suffered because of their participation in Security Council sanctions. The discussion of adverse, unintended consequences focused almost exclusively on economic impacts, not on the situation of average citizens living within a targeted state.

It did not occur to policy makers or analysts early in the decade that the unintended impacts of sanctions would harm those very social sectors within a targeted country that might be most supportive of the norms being protected by the UN Security Council. Consideration of these matters was somewhat skewed by the experience of South Africa, where the African National Congress supported economic sanctions even while acknowledging their deleterious effect on the majority population. By the decade's end, it was clear that sanctions carried with them the potential for bitter irony: often imposed to prevent human rights abuse and lawlessness, sanctions sometimes strengthened the centralised control of repressive regimes. At times they also disempowered those who were opposing from within policies that were being subjected to isolation from without.

By the end of the decade, decision makers and scholars alike embarked on a search for ways to increase the political effectiveness of sanctions while reducing unintended negative consequences.

The resulting quest for targeted, or "smart", sanctions dominated the discussion of sanctions policy and led to intensive efforts by member states and the UN Secretariat to develop more precise and selective forms of economic coercion.

3. The UN system lacks the ability to administer sanctions.

Throughout the 1990s the Security Council had to improvise mechanisms to impose, administer and monitor sanctions effectively. The sanctions committees established in each case to oversee implementation varied in effectiveness according to the degree of politicisation of the particular episode, its relative importance for the major powers and the leadership provided by the committee chairs. But in all cases the United Nations' ability to enforce sanctions was woefully inadequate. In an era of financial constraint at the United Nations, the Security Council and its sanctions committees lacked sufficient resources to evaluate and implement sanctions.

A substantial amount of learning and adaptation occurred during the past decade as the UN system began to find other innovative approaches to improving implementation. Sanctions became more tightly focused, had clearer objectives and even began to feature pre-assessments of likely impacts. Strategies for mitigating adverse humanitarian impacts on vulnerable populations were incorporated into sanctions policies and considered essential for their success. At the policy level, a variety of creative proposals circulated by the end of the decade for better targeting of sanctions. The most important of these was the two-year initiative of the Swiss government, the Interlaken process, which produced serious and far-reaching proposals for refining targeted financial sanctions. In April 2000 the Security Council established a sanctions reform working group to recommend specific changes in UN policies and procedures. One of the issues the council sought to address in these efforts was how to end sanctions in cases of partial or ambiguous compliance. Thus, the concept of "suspension" emerged as a halfway point between continuing and ending sanctions. This may be a precursor to the development of other concepts and strategies that permit greater bargaining within a sanctions environment.

4. There are tensions between the goals of the Security Council and those of member states

Early in the decade Lisa Martin published a detailed theoretical study demonstrating that the co-operation sustaining sanctions tends to change among states as the sanctions episode progresses.[1] Larger and more powerful states, especially the five permanent members of the Security Council, have tended historically to steer or capture the sanctions enterprise to meet their particular foreign policy objectives, which may or may not match the goals of the broader UN community. The history of the Iraqi and Libyan cases in particular reflects tensions between UN objectives and those of major states such as the United States and Great Britain.

5. Sanctions are sometimes used as an alternative or prelude to war.

For many member states and UN officials, the attraction of sanctions lies in their potential utility as an alternative way of responding to threats to peace. They comprise a middle ground between doing nothing and authorising the use of military force. Others view sanctions as a peaceful means of coercion or as a powerful means of persuasion but, in any case, as an alternative to the use of force. Under this rubric, sanctions were not to be followed by the use of force. In the cases of Iraq, Haiti and Yugoslavia, however, sanctions gave way to military force, with the conclusion easily derived from the first two cases that military force accomplished what sanctions could not. Some analysts suggested that sanctions seemed to be used as a way of softening public opinion for the subsequent use of force, as a first step toward war that crippled the targeted economy and psychologically intimidated its population.

Apart from this debate on intentionality in the use of sanctions, it is important to recognise that sanctions are extreme measures that can have effects in some cases equal to or more severe than those of war. The perception of sanctions as a peaceful or "soft" tool of persuasion does not reflect the harsh reality of the economic and social devastation that can result, especially from general trade sanctions. Sanctions are often a biting means of economic coercion and need to be understood as instruments of forceful diplomacy. As one sanctions committee chairperson noted to us, the best understanding of sanctions may be that they are three-quarters of the way toward the use of force, and that they may have their greatest impact when it is clear to the targeted state that the imposers will resort to military force if sanctions fail to achieve their stated goal.

[...]

Unintended Political Effects

The cases of the past decade reveal that sanctions can be self-defeating in the domestic political arena, which is especially troublesome when sanctions are imposed to restore democracy and improve human rights. To some extent negative unintended consequences may be unavoidable. But the Security Council should make every possible effort to ensure that any sanctions it imposes do not unduly victimise or harm the interests of reform groups or opposition constituencies within a targeted regime that support the very norms the United Nations is seeking to uphold.

Despite its limited capacity to administer sanctions effectively, the United Nations was given the task of managing the twelve sanctions cases of the 1990s. In the process the UN system gained valuable experience about the institutional structures and policies that contribute to effectiveness. Although each case unfolded under very diverse circumstances, with differing structural arrangements, some generalisations flow from these experiences:

- Swift, forceful sanctions tend to be more effective than slow, incremental measures.

- With greater co-operation from front-line states and the major trading partners of the target, sanctions will be more successful.

- When a sanctions committee is more engaged, as evidenced by frequency of meetings and the active role of its chair, implementation will be enhanced.

- A greater effort devoted to sanctions monitoring, both regarding violations and political and humanitarian impacts, will produce more effective sanctions.

- The involvement of regional organisations can greatly enhance sanctions implementation.

Each of these findings warrants amplification, as detailed briefly below:

The Scope and Intensity of Sanctions

The cases of the past decade illustrate that the effectiveness of sanctions depends greatly on swift and forceful implementation. This finding confirms the conclusion reached in the original IIE study of 1990 that swift and comprehensive measures are most effective, but does not deny the value of ratcheting up pressure in cases in which previous sanctions have not been sufficient to induce policy change.[2] In the Yugoslavia case, the progressive strengthening of measures in Resolution 787 (1992) and 820 (1993) contributed to the effectiveness of sanctions as bargaining leverage on the Milosevic regime. Nor does this emphasis on swift and forceful imposition deny the importance of inducement strategies as part of the sanctions-generated bargaining dynamic. Offering rewards for compliance can produce positive reciprocity and enhance the effectiveness of the bargaining process. The combination of forceful sanctions and concrete incentives for compliance can be highly effective.

The Yugoslavia case illustrates the effectiveness of ratcheting down pressure as an inducement for greater compliance. The lack of such inducements in the Iraq case, by contrast, impeded the prospects for greater compliance. Although the United Nations is limited in the incentives it can offer (lacking financial resources and the ability to provide security assurances), the Security Council can offer a very significant inducement—the lifting or suspending of sanctions. The cases of the past decade show that the desire for a lifting of sanctions is a priority for most targeted regimes. The effective use of this potential reward is crucial to successful bargaining dynamics.

One of the creative inducement concepts that developed in UN circles with regard to the Iraq and Libyan episodes was the notion of sanctions suspension. Rather than raising the issue of an end to sanctions, which would have forced an acrimonious debate within the Security Council, some member states proposed instead a suspension of sanctions. Although some questioned the difference between termination and suspension, arguing that it was only a matter of semantics, for UN diplomats the distinction was important. The latter term implied the maintenance of some sanctions controls and an ability to bargain with a targeted state regarding its continued compliance.

Member State Co-operation

The co-operation of a targeted regime's neighbouring states and principal trading partners is essential. In many of the cases in Africa, where neighbouring states were either unwilling or unable to co-operate with UN sanctions, sanctions were completely ineffective. In Haiti the lack of compliance by the Dominican Republic weakened the impact of sanctions. The problem of non-co-operation is largely a political question, arising from the disagreement of neighbouring states with the UN agenda, but it is also a structural issue. The lack of legal, administrative and institutional capacity for sanctions implementation among many member states is a major impediment to political effectiveness.

The two cases with the greatest degree of co-operation from neighbouring states, Iraq and Yugoslavia, were also the most successful cases. Compliance in the Iraq case was greatly aided by the co-operation of Turkey, a part of the US-led coalition, and Iran, Iraq's military adversary. The special arrangement allowing Iraq to export oil to Jordan also played an important role. In the case of Yugoslavia, the extensive monitoring and enforcement effort mounted by European regional institutions was decisive in applying economic pressure to Belgrade.

However, where regional organisations lack sufficient resources, their ability to enhance sanctions implementation is limited. In Liberia and Sierra Leone, the Economic Community of West African States (Ecowas) established regional monitoring and enforcement efforts aided by its military arm, Ecomog. But these efforts were hampered by an emphasis on military operations and a lack of infrastructure and institutional capacity for customs control and border monitoring. In the Sierra Leone case, the UN sanctions committee in New York maintained liaison with Ecowas, and the Office for the Co-ordination of Humanitarian Affairs provided support for the monitoring of humanitarian relief. Although this assistance was minimal and came too late in the short-lived sanctions effort to have much impact, it could serve as a model for recognising and supporting the implementation efforts of regional organisations in less developed areas of the world.

Administrative Structures

The role of sanctions committees and the associated administrative structure in the UN Secretariat can affect the implementation of sanctions and the administration of humanitarian relief. The most effective sanctions, those imposed on Iraq and Yugoslavia, had the most active and engaged sanctions committees. The Iraq committee, in particular, was constantly involved in a wide range of activities, especially the processing of humanitarian exemption applications. The oil-for-food programme implemented in 1996 became a huge operation with a substantial bureaucratic apparatus. By the end of the 1990s the budget for the UN Iraq programme grew to more than $10 billion per year, exceeding that of the United Nations itself.

The oil-for-food programme itself was unique owing to the combination of the humanitarian crisis related to the sanctions and the ability of Iraq to generate huge oil revenues to pay for the needed supplies. The presence of cash-generating oil exports gave the Security Council inventive possibilities for dealing with the humanitarian crisis. Very few instances are likely to arise in which the sanctioned nation will be able or willing to pay for offsetting its own economic strangulation.

One of the more remarkable features of the Iraqi sanctions was the manner in which so many member states, including those who became vocal in their opposition to the continuation of sanctions in the latter half of the decade, nonetheless maintained the embargo. This was due in part to the relative ease of enforcing the oil embargo, especially when key neighbouring countries remained committed to keeping the pipelines shut.

In many of the cases in which sanctions were ineffective, the sanctions committees played little or no role. In the Somalia case, the oversight effort was so minimal that the Security Council had to adopt a special resolution (Resolution 954 in 1994) requesting that the sanctions committee fulfil its duties. In the Liberia and Rwanda cases as well, the sanctions committees played little or no role in attempting to implement the arms embargoes. The limitations of these sanctions regimes were reflected in the inactivity of the associated sanctions committees.

In the Angola case, as the Security Council strengthened sanctions measures in 1997 and 1998, the sanctions committee became more active and attempted to play a more assertive role in encouraging compliance with the sanctions, especially among neighbouring states in Africa. Committee chair Robert Fowler, permanent representative of Canada to the Security Council, made an innovative effort in 1999 and 2000 to mobilise support for the sanctions. The convening of expert panels by the Angola committee, following the example of the Iraq committee, marked another creative attempt by the sanctions committee to enhance monitoring and effectiveness. However, whether these efforts by the Angola committee will result in greater co-operation with sanctions among member states and ultimately bring about some compliance by the targeted Unita regime remains to be seen.

Monitoring Is Essential

One of the most significant developments in sanctions enforcement over the past decade was the introduction of sanctions assistance missions (SAMs) to monitor and enforce the sanctions against Yugoslavia. SAMs were the most elaborate and highly developed monitoring programme ever established. Western European governments sent customs officers to the countries surrounding Yugoslavia, and the Western European Union and the North Atlantic Treaty Organisation established patrol missions on the Danube and in the Adriatic. The SAMs contributed significantly to the success of the sanctions against Belgrade, making them the most rigorously enforced in history.

In other cases, the lack of anything resembling SAMs among regional organisations meant that implementation efforts were either limited or non-existent. When the Organisation of American States imposed sanctions against Haiti in 1991, it had no means of assuring the implementation of these measures. When Ecowas imposed sanctions against Liberia and Sierra Leone, it created sanctions committees to monitor and enforce these measures, but the committees lacked the necessary financial resources and technical capacity to ensure effective implementation. Regional organisations can and must play a central role in the monitoring and enforcement of sanctions, but the realisation of this potential will depend on the greater availability of financial and technical resources and a stronger political commitment to the objectives of UN sanctions.

Seeing Beyond Iraq

In part because no comparative and summary assessment of UN-imposed multilateral sanctions has been undertaken until now, the conclusions and findings offered here are tentative in nature. Nonetheless, certain patterns of experience and policy trends have become clear during the past decade. One of the challenges has been to see beyond the Iraq case. The debate over Iraq has so dominated the discourse on sanctions that it has skewed public understanding of the real data of sanctions and the successful adaptations that have occurred in recent years. The UN community has learned a great deal more about the conditions under which sanctions are successful than the general debate on these questions might suggest. The understanding of humanitarian and social consequences resulting from sanctions has also expanded. By drawing on the experience of the past decade and gleaning appropriate lessons from both the successes and failures, scholars and policy makers now know a great deal more than they did previously about he ways to mitigate adverse humanitarian consequences and about the factors that can contribute to policy effectiveness.

Endnotes

1. Lisa L. Martin, Coercive Cooperation: Explaining Multilateral Economic Sanctions (Princeton, N.J.: Princeton University Press, 1992).
2. Hufbauer, Schott and Elliott, Economic Sanctions Reconsidered, pp. 100-2.

US Sanctions Are a Means To an End, Not an End Unto Themselves

Bryan Early

In the following excerpted viewpoint, Bryan Early argues that the United States employs economic sanctions too often and without fully acknowledging their downsides. He suggests that policymakers consider the prospective costs and negative impacts of sanctions, and adapt policies that reflect thought without jumping the gun. Early is an Associate Professor of Political Science and Director of the Center for Policy Research and Project on International Security, Commerce, and Economic Statecraft (PISCES) at the University of Albany's Rockefeller College of Public Affairs and Policy. He conducts research on topics related to foreign policy, strategic trade controls, and the proliferation of nuclear and aerospace technology.

As you read, consider the following questions:

1. Why is the threat of sanctions sometime most effective?
2. What three conditions should politicians regularly evaluate on imposed sanctions?
3. According to the author, in what ways do economic sanctions suffer from flawed implementation?

Policymakers employ economic sanctions far more than they should and often without fully appreciating the downsides to their use. While economic sanctions can appear like an

"Statecraft and the Limitations of Economic Sanctions", by Bryan Early, E-International Relations, August 21, 2016. http://www.e-ir.info/2016/08/21/statecraft-and-the-limitations-of-economic-sanctions/. Licensed under CC BY-NC 4.0 International.

attractive alternative to military force, they are not well-suited for accomplishing many foreign policy objectives. There are also a number of substantial and frequently intractable impediments that prevent economic sanctions from succeeding. Additionally, there are multiple pathologies associated with why policymakers sometimes choose to adopt sanctions and why ineffective sanctions are left in place. By employing sanctions either too quickly or remaining overly committed to sanctions-based diplomatic strategies, policymakers can make bad situations worse or forgo opportunities to make bad situations better.

No other country employs economic sanctions more than the United States. The US Government employs sanctions to curb nuclear proliferation, stop human rights abuses, encourage democratization, disrupt conflicts, and eliminate unfair trade practices. Whereas some of its sanctions achieve their goals in a matter of months or years, other US sanctioning efforts have lingered on unsuccessfully decades. Using the most optimistic of benchmarks, US economic sanctions are only successful around a third of the time (Hufbauer, Schott, Elliot, and Oegg 2007). In pursuing US foreign policy interests, policymakers should be cautious in employing sanctions, circumspect in their expectations for success, and remember than sanctions are a means to end not an end unto themselves.

[...]

Effective Sanctions versus Effective Sanctions Policies

Policymakers can make their sanctioning strategies more effective and less costly, but there are some tradeoffs between the two. The most effective economic sanctions are often the ones that never get imposed. It has been found that threatening sanctions can sometime succeed at obtaining concessions without having to follow through on them. Rather than imposing sanctions right away, governments are often best served by levelling sanctions threats first (Drezner 2003; Bapat et al. 2013). This strategy is a particularly cost-effective form of coercion as it can allow the government to achieve its goals without having to bear the costs of imposing the sanctions. For threats to be effective, though, they must be both costly and credible. This means that the governments issuing such threats have to demonstrate their willingness to adopt costly sanctions and rarely back away from the threats they have issued in order for their threats to be taken seriously (Peterson 2013). To maximize the general likelihood that targets will concede to sanctions threats, sender states may have to follow through in imposing sanctions that are likely to be both costly and ineffective to demonstrate their threats' credibility. Policymakers should thus employ sanctions threats sparingly and primarily when they are willing to follow through on whatever threats they level.

Having committed to imposing economic sanctions and decided upon their scope and severity, there still remains a lot of work to be done in imposing sanctions. Effectively implementing economic sanctions can require substantial investments of governmental resources (Morgan and Bapat 2003). Governments must publicize the sanctions to their relevant industries, education about what the compliance requirements are, and the invest resources in monitoring and enforcing compliance (Early 2016). If economic sanctions exist only on paper, then they are not likely to be effective.

Leaders should also consistently evaluate whether their economic sanctions are having the intended effects, whether continuing to impose them is worth the costs, and whether sanctions remain a better option than alternative strategies. Economic sanctions sometimes can take years to work, but if they are allowed to persist longer than dozen years they almost never succeed. Policymakers should regularly evaluate whether it is best to maintain existing sanctions, enhance them, or abandon them in light of their prospective costs and odds of success. Problematically, policymakers can sometimes get tunnel vision with respect to sanctions in which they perceive the only option for addressing their ineffectiveness is to escalate the sanctions' severity. Research has shown, though, that gradually increasing the severity of sanctions is not nearly as effective as imposing very harsh, disruptive sanctions all at once (Hufbauer et al. 2007). If economic sanctions appear unlikely to work, as is the case when target states have established extensive sanctions-busting relationships (Early 2015), policymakers are often best served by giving up on sanctions or, at the very least, beginning to pursue other forms of engagement.

In the case of the US sanctioning effort against Cuba initiated in 1960, for example, Cuba secured extensive foreign assistance from the Soviet Union shortly after the sanctions were imposed in addition to forging trade-based sanctions-busting with a number of the United States' commercial competitors. Following the Cold War's conclusion, Cuba was able to obtain the patronage of both Venezuela and China—while expanding its trade relationships with many European states, Canada, and Mexico. US efforts to escalate its sanctions against Cuba in the 1990s constituted a major failure (Early 2015). Only recently has the Obama Administration sought a different course by making robust diplomatic entreaties with Cuba and relaxing at least some of the sanctions restrictions. After five-plus decades of relying almost exclusively on sanctions, the US Government is finally pursuing a broader set of policies more likely to yield meaningful reforms in Cuba. At the very least, President Obama's strategy has initiated a renaissance in Cuban-American relations that had been antagonistic for half a century—and even after the Cold War had concluded.

Knowing when to remain committed to economic sanctions versus giving up or pursuing other policy options is by no means an easy task. A good heuristic, though, is that policymakers should generally consider giving up on sanctioning efforts that have not worked after a decade—either by abandoning the goals being pursued or by adopting alternative policy options to achieve them. Once sanctions have persisted beyond ten years, it's difficult to credit them with success in achieving their goals or to necessarily justify their accumulated costs.

The recent set of democratizing reforms taking place in Myanmar are a good example of how US economic sanctions may be associated with the achievement of their goals but may not have much to do with their acquisition. The US Government first sanctioned Myanmar (then called Burma) back in 1988 after its military-led government lethally cracked down on democratic protests. The military-led regime remained in power, nullifying the results of the 1990 election in which the opposition party (the National League for Democracy) won over 80 percent of the seats in parliament and imprisoning many of its members. Myanmar's government continued to engage in host of politically repressive and human rights-abusing policies for more than twenty years. From 1990-2011, Freedom House (2016) assigned Myanmar its lowest scores possible on both its measures of political rights and civil liberties. According to Wood and Gibney's (2010) Political Terror Scores, the Myanmar Government engaged in civil and political rights violations that affected most or the entirety of the country during this period. In the midst of this period, the US Government strengthened its sanctions against Myanmar in 1997 by banning US investments in the country as a result of the "severe repression" of the country's population (Hadar 1998). These sanctions did not cause any improvement in Myanmar's political or human rights policies over the ensuing decade.

In the fall of 2009, the Obama Administration decided to adopt a new strategy that focused on direct diplomatic engagement with Myanmar's ruling regime and limited cooperation in areas of mutual interest. At least initially, President Obama left the existing sanctions in place. Shortly thereafter, Myanmar's military regime initiated a set of transformative changes to its political policies. It held open elections, released political prisoners, and respected the results of the election won by the opposition through the formation of a "quasi-civilian government" (Martin 2013: 1-2). This included the release of Nobel Peace Prize winner Aung San Suu Kyi, who had spent 15 years under house arrest due to her involvement in Myanmar's political opposition. She was allowed to run for the parliament in 2012 and became Myanmar's State Counsellor in 2015. Certainly, the Obama Administration has used the relaxation of sanctions as tool for supporting and encouraging Myanmar's democratization. Yet, it was the Obama Administration's diplomatic engagement rather than US sanctions that was the major catalyst for change. If anything, US economic sanctions were most strongly associated with the Myanmar regime's most brutal periods of repression rather than forcing the regime to reform or respect its citizens' human rights. Just because US economic sanctions were in place against Myanmar when the regime initiated political reforms does not mean the sanctions achieved the goals for which they were imposed 20-plus years earlier. Rather than being a sanctions success story, the best that can be said for the sanctions is that they have played a partially constructive, secondary role in incentivizing political change in Myanmar after more than two decades of failure.

Economic Sanctions, the Goldilocks Trap, and Policy Inertia

Despite their limited chances of success and potential to be counterproductive, US policymakers still continue to rely on economic sanctions more than any other country in the world. Why? A large part of that answer likely lies in the nature of policy options that policymakers have in dealing with international disputes and crises (Baldwin 1999). Doing nothing may often be an unattractive option because it can make leaders appear weak, indecisive, or apathetic. Offering no response also limits the likelihood of a bad situation improving. Diplomatic responses may also be viewed as insufficient, especially if initial diplomatic entreaties have failed to resolve the issue. On the other end of the spectrum, threatening or employing military force may be too risky or too costly to consider. Using military force for certain objectives may also be inappropriate or unjustifiable.

Economic sanctions are often viewed as occupying the middle-ground between diplomacy and military force. Just like Goldilocks considering which porridge option best-suited her palette, policymakers often decide that the most attractive policy falls in between a cold war of words and a hot conflict. This is aided by the fact that economic sanctions tend to be easy for policymakers to adopt, either through executive order or legislation. As described above, a key challenge with respect to economic sanctions resides in their implementation and the policymakers that decide to impose sanctions often have little to do with following through on their implementation.

Contributing to the problem is that, whereas policymakers can be criticized for doing nothing, offering only "empty" words, or for the fallout of military actions gone awry, policymakers are almost never held liable for ineffective sanctions policies. Part of this stems from the long time lines that required to judge sanctions' effectiveness. It also relates to the difficulty of evaluating the full set of costs associated with imposing economic sanctions and the cumulative set of negative externalities they have. By the time that the full set of costs and consequences from failed sanctions policies can be fully evaluated, the policymakers that made those decisions and the public's attention will have often already moved on. All this can help make sanctions appear to be the most expedient, low-risk, "just right" option available to policymakers. Again and again, that's a large part of why policymakers keep gravitating back to economic sanctions in order to address their foreign policy problems.

Another pathology relates to when sanctions policies become accepted as the status quo government policy towards a particular target. With regard to government policies, it's always much harder to adopt new policies than to let old ones persist. Economic sanctions can accumulate entrenched interests that benefit from maintaining the status quo. In the case of the US sanctions against Cuba, for example, the US sugar industry has benefited enormously from the embargo against Cuban sugar imports. For the sugar industry, the embargo serves as a projectionist benefit that keeps the price of US sugar higher than it otherwise would be and it has lobbied to keep the sanctions in place. The politics surrounding the removal of sanctions can be politically contentious for non-economic reasons as well. The American-Israeli Political Action Committee (AIPAC), for example, strongly lobbied Congress to block President Obama's efforts at offering sanctions relief negotiated as part of the JCPOA with Iran. The US "State Sponsors of Terrorism" list subject to mandatory sanctions represents another good example of the inertia that sanctions can take on. Once a country gets on that list, getting off of it can be incredibly difficult for governments to do even if they have clearly stopped supporting terrorism. Sanctions written into legislative statute are the hardest to remove. Governments and, in particular, the United States can thus become locked-in to sanctions-dominated foreign policy strategies even if they no longer appear to be effective. Policymakers may thus lose out on otherwise promising opportunities to resolve disputes or find compromises because sanctions get in the way of rather than facilitating positive outcomes.

Economic Sanctions and Smarter Statecraft

As this essay has shown, there are significant challenges in employing economic sanctions successfully under optimal circumstances and there are a myriad of reasons why economic sanctions might suffer from flawed implementation. The major criticisms highlighted above can be summarized as follows:

- Economic sanctions face numerous significant and often intractable barriers to achieving their political goals

- Imposing economic sanctions can entail significant, but difficult to estimate economic costs for their senders and also have a broad range of adverse, unintended consequences

- Policymakers often employ economic sanctions for reasons other than their prospects for success

- Once imposed, it can be very difficult for policymakers to break away from sanctions-based foreign policy strategies

Together, these findings suggest that policymakers should approach the use of economic sanctions much more carefully than they presently do. Imposing economic sanctions may appear like an attractive option for reasons other than their likelihood of success, but that is often because so many of their adverse consequences can be difficult to assess prior to their imposition. This does not mean that economic sanctions cannot play a useful role in states' foreign policies altogether, but that how policymakers use sanctions should change.

Policymakers should give more careful consideration to economic sanctions' prospective costs and negative externalities, limit the use of sanctions to the circumstances in which they are most appropriate, and subject ongoing sanctioning efforts to regular evaluations regarding the benefits of maintaining them. The new wave of research on sanctions' externalities suggests that policymakers can potentially account for the unintended effects that their economic sanctions will have on the behavior their targets. Econometric forecasting models can also be used to estimate the projected domestic economic costs of imposing sanctions, both immediately and into the future. By incorporating a broader scope analysis of the total range of costs associated with economic sanctions, policymakers can better evaluate whether non-instrumental, immediate benefits of imposing sanctions are worth the longer range costs. Policymakers should also factor in the extent to which economic sanctions are actually conducive to achieving those goals. In the case of promoting human rights, for example, sanctions may not be appropriate. Finally, policymakers should be cognizant that economic sanctions polices can take on a life of their own. This should give policymakers pause in whether imposing them is warranted, but they can also adopt provisions that subject sanctions policies to period review. One approach would be to build in long-term sunset clauses into sanctions legislation. While a short-term sunset clause might cause the targets of sanctions to question the sender's resolve, a sunset clause that forced the sanctions to be actively renewed after 10 years could be useful.

Another important insight from this essay is that strategies relying on the pure coercive nature of economic sanctions rarely succeed in their goals. In the cases of the US sanctions against

Cuba, Myanmar, and Iran, overcoming the antagonism that had built up over decades-worth of sanctions required active diplomatic outreach. In the cases of Cuba and Myanmar, the Obama Administration combined bold diplomacy with promises of relaxing sanctions in order to improve relations and start down the path of achieving the sanctions' goals. Sanctions alone, however, were not capable of forcing either country to make the desired concessions. After decades of ineffective sanctions against Iran, the US was able to forge a strong multilateral coalition that supported the sanctioning effort against Iran at beginning of the Obama Administration. Rather than trying force Iran into making unilateral concessions, though, President Obama used those sanctions to bring Iran to the bargaining table and negotiate from a position of strength. Imposing economic sanctions is easy, but making them actually work—especially on their own—is hard. Policymakers should avoid narrowly committing themselves to sanctions-based foreign policy strategies without regularly considering other options for engagement.

Economic sanctions will continue to be used irrespective of whatever critiques are made against them because of how easily and expediently policymakers can employ them to "do something" in response in response to foreign policy challenges. Economic sanctions provide policymakers with a potentially useful alternative to military force when coercive statecraft is warranted, but they are associated with their own set of unique challenges, costs, and risks. Even compared to the use of military force, economic sanctions are not always the least costly option, especially in the long-term, and they are associated with numerous pathologies that can limit their effectiveness and even make them counterproductive. US policymakers, in particular, should be mindful of the perils of overly relying on economic sanctions and exercise significant discretion in their use.

Sanctions Are the Least Effective Method for Change

Hannah Tucker Warren

In the following excerpted viewpoint, Hannah Tucker Warren argues that economic sanctions are not only ineffective in changing the target state's behavior, but sanctions punish multinational corporations by losing market share to foreign companies. She evaluates the US sanctions imposed on Russia in hopes of pressuring Putin to reverse his annexation of Crimea and to withdraw Russian troops and its support of rebels in eastern Ukraine. Warren is a Judicial Law Clerk at Western District of Texas. She holds a J.D. from the University of Houston Law Center.

As you read, consider the following questions:

1. According to Robert Pape, what three criteria should sanctions meet in order to be considered effective?
2. How are sanctions imposed on Cuba similar and dissimilar to sanctions imposed on Russian?
3. Who does the Takings Clause protect and why?

W estern sanctions against Russia are costing America's most powerful company a few hundred million bucks. A billion to be exact." Historically, sanctions have been considered one of the least effective methods for inciting change. Why, then, have

"The New Cold War: A Novel Regulatory Takings Theory on Economic Sanctions Against Exploration and Production in Russia," by Hannah Tucker Warren, Houston Journal of International Law, June 12, 2017. Reprinted by permission.

sanctions increasingly been a foreign policy tool of choice in the face of a slow American economy and an ever-competitive oil and gas market?

Economic Sanctions

Economic sanctions are "deliberate government-inspired withdrawal, or threat of withdrawal, of customary trade or financial relations." They are imposed for reasons ranging from stopping nuclear proliferations to promoting peaceful and democratic change. Currently, Western sanctions against Russia aim to punish the participants of a militarized dispute—that is, the hostile takeover of Crimea from the sovereign Ukraine.

[...]

Economic Sanctions on Russia

On March 6, 2014, in response to Russia's illegal annexation of Crimea, President Barack Obama, acting under IEEPA, declared a national emergency, blocked specific Russian nationals from transferring their respective property and interests in property subject to the jurisdiction of the United States, and authorized the Secretary of the Treasury to promulgate regulations carrying out Executive Order 13360. As support for his Order, President Obama cited the "actions and policies of persons . . . who have asserted governmental authority in the Crimean region without the authorization of the Government of Ukraine," which "undermin[ed] democratic processes" and "threaten[ed] [Ukraine's] peace, security, stability, sovereignty, and territorial integrity." Effective on May 8, 2014, the Secretary issued the Ukraine-Related Sanctions Regulations, which prohibits all transactions defined by Executive Orders 13660, 13661, and 13662, and mandates that any US person holding targeted funds place such funds "in a blocked interest-bearing account located in the United States." The European Union, United Nations, and several other countries followed suit and implemented their own sanctioning regimes.

The conflict in Ukraine is rooted in Slavic history and ongoing sociopolitical turmoil. Even before the Crimean annexation, Ukraine has been plagued by a cultural divide between the northern region, anchored by the westernized city of Kiev, and the southeastern region, which is predominately populated by ethnic Russians. After years of corruption, slow economic growth, and a struggle to be more closely aligned with the European Union, Ukrainian government officials sought out an EU Association Agreement that would establish a political and economic association between the parties, securing judicial and financial reforms for Ukraine and ensuring natural gas imports to the greater European Union.

The city of Kiev erupted in protests after now-former Ukrainian President Viktor Yanukovych refused to sign the Agreement and instead signed a treaty and multi-billion-dollar loan with long-time friend, President Vladimir Putin. The protests grew into what is now named the Ukrainian Revolution, or "Euromaidan," resulting in violent clashes between law enforcement and protestors in sub-zero temperatures. After several days of protesting, Ukrainians effectively ousted Yanukovych, who fled the country to Russia and has not since returned. Soon thereafter, the newly appointed interim government signed the Association Agreement in exchange for committing to adopt broad reforms.

In response to the Ukrainian Revolution, pro-Russian demonstrations were held in the southeastern city of Sevastopol. The pro-Russian demonstrations culminated in the Russian takeover of the Supreme Council of Crimea, the capture of several strategic sites across Crimea, and ultimately the annexation of the Republic of Crimea and the city of Sevastopol. The Western world has refused to recognize the annexation of Crimea.

The US government immediately responded to the annexation with sanctions. On March 6, 2014, President Obama signed Executive Order 13660, authorizing sanctions on individuals and entities responsible for violating the sovereignty and territorial integrity of Ukraine, or for stealing the assets of Ukrainian people. On April 28, 2014, the United States imposed a second round of sanctions, banning seven Russian officials—including

Igor Sechin, the executive chairman of Rosneft, Russia's leading petroleum company—from conducting business transactions with US persons or within the United States. On July 16, 2014, the United States further extended sanctions to ban Russian energy firms Rosneft and Novatek, as well as two banks, Gazprombank and Vnesheconombank (VEB). The fourth round of sanctions, administered on September 11, 2014, directly targeted Russia's financial, energy, and defense sectors.

In short, "[n]o US oil company can do business with Russia," no US companies can "sell drilling technology [to Russia] to access oil and gas reserves," and no US banks can "issue long-term loans to Russian businesses for energy-focused projects." "By targeting individuals and companies in oil field services, the sanctions could slow capital investments in Russia's oil sector and affect future output." This would have a larger impact for the US oil and gas industry over the long-term, as "Russia produces some 10 million of the about 90 million barrels of oil pumped daily around the world." To put this into perspective, "[i]f oil and natural gas are considered together, Russia is the world's largest energy-exporting country, surpassing even Saudi Arabia."

The goal of these sanctions is to weaken Russia's economy "in hopes the pressure will entice Putin, over time, to reverse his annexation of Crimea and to withdraw Russian troops and its support of rebels in eastern Ukraine." Recently, however, Secretary of State (and former CEO of ExxonMobil) Rex Tillerson said that US sanctions imposed against Russia will "remain in place until Russia returns control of the peninsula to Ukraine." Ultimately, as will be further explained in the following section, the executive branch must delicately balance the sanctions regime against the effect on a sluggish oil and gas industry and a dependence on "imported energy in spite of rising domestic output."

[…]

The United States is not in a war with Russia, like it was with Iraq when President George W. Bush first issued sanctions in 2003, nor in a demonstrated hostile situation like it was with Iran and their proliferation of nuclear power. Economic sanctions against Russia are arguably more about the feared reunification of a Soviet bloc regime and trying to strong-arm President Putin. Since the initial writing of this Comment, a report by the US Intelligence Community has suggested with high confidence that Russian President Vladimir Putin "ordered an influence campaign in 2016 aimed at the US presidential election." Strikingly similar to the support for the Ukraine-Related Sanctions, the intelligence assessment found that "Russia's goals were to undermine public faith in the US democratic process," in addition to diminishing Hillary Clinton's electability. While the judgments from this report have not been included in this analysis of the novel takings claim, the report would greatly support not finding a taking because the public interest in protecting against interference in US democratic elections would be unquestionably outweighed by the private harm of prohibiting corporate investment in Russia.

[…]

A more structured level of analysis is needed to evaluate the effectiveness of the Ukraine-Related Sanctions. Robert Pape explains that

> economic sanctions should be credited with success if they meet three criteria: (1) the target state conceded to a significant part of the coercer's demands; (2) economic sanctions were threatened or actually applied before the target changed its behavior; and (3) no more-credible explanation exists for the target's change of behavior.

The simplest way to evaluate the effectiveness under Pape's structure is to argue that Russia has not—and will not—concede to US demands to restore Crimea to Ukraine. Even looking past the more obvious goal, it is still not clear whether there has been any successful behavior modification as a result of the sanctions, though it may be too early to tell.

Others would argue, however, that sanctions are generally ineffective and are especially ineffective in the case against Russia. Drawing parallels to sanctions against Cuba is useful to illustrate

Russia Retaliates For Sanctions

Russia's foreign ministry on Friday announced counter measures in response to tough new sanctions proposed by the United States, ordering Washington to reduce its diplomatic staff.

Moscow ordered the US to reduce its diplomatic presence in Russia to 455 diplomats and staff and also barred it from using a Moscow summer house and storage facility.

The ministry said that this was in response to the passing of a new bill on sanctions by the Senate late Thursday. US President Donald Trump will now have to decide whether to accept or veto the measures.

President Vladimir Putin on Thursday slammed what he called "anti-Russian hysteria" in Washington and said that Russia could not "endlessly tolerate this kind of insolence."

Moscow complained that the "new sanctions bill showed with all clarity that relations with Russia have fallen hostage to the domestic political struggle in the US."

It warned that it "reserves the right to carry out other measures that could affect the interests of the US" while acting in a reciprocal fashion.

The move comes after Russia has repeatedly expressed anger at Washington barring its diplomats access to two compounds in the US in December last year, under Barack Obama, in response to suspected Russian meddling in the US election.

Obama at the same time expelled 35 Russian diplomats for spying.

President Vladimir Putin initially held off from retaliating, saying he would wait to see how Trump reacted after he came into the White House.

"Russia orders the US to cut its diplomatic staff in retaliation for sanctions," by Mikhail Klimentyev, Public Radio International, July 28, 2017.

why. While this Comment does not purport to review the amalgam of literature evaluating the effectiveness of the US sanctions on Cuba, the mass of evidence suggests that punishment has not caused Cuba to change. Rather, it has given Cuba's regime a plausible excuse for further repressing the liberties of individual Cubans. It is important to understand the context in which the economic sanctions, or negative incentives, are imposed. Cubans, like Russians, do not have a democratic tradition to which they long to return. Also, both populations traditionally did not have access to economic opportunity or to the markets. Therefore, the "punishment" of not interacting with the United States may not seem overwhelmingly burdensome after all.

On the other hand, lack of interaction with sanctioning nations, namely the United States and the European Union, may push Russia to interact with non-sanctioning nations, such as China. Major players in the oil and gas industry are already seeing this happen. It does not help that "[d]emand for energy in Asia is projected to grow at an annual rate of two and a half percent through 2035, a level that is almost double that of the rest of the world." To sweeten the deal, China is "willing to provide loans or make prepayments that provide Russia's often debt-ridden energy companies with ready cash to start building pipelines and modernize their production at low financial risk." An agreement between China National Petroleum Corporation (CNPC) and Gazprom, securing "a thirty-year, $400 billion deal that will result in up to thirty-eight billion cubic meters (bcm) of Russian gas going to China annually," is the kind of thing that diminishes any remaining value for US players.

Finding alternative outlets or turning to new markets also occurred when Western sanctions were levied on Cuba, which became a close ally and client of the Soviet Union, acting in accordance with the Soviet Union's wishes rather than its own. This would suggest that economic sanction regimes do not encourage positive change, but instead discourage or preclude it. While it is true, as Andrea Ovan suggests in her recent article in the Harvard Business Review, that "trade war is better than a nuclear war," some argue that "sanctions still have a long way to go in becoming an overtly successful foreign policy tool."

The Takings Clause is "designed to bar Government from forcing some people alone to bear public burdens which, in all fairness and justice, should be borne by the public as a whole." ExxonMobil has not borne the burden of economic sanctions on its own—the effects of sanctions are felt by many American businesses that operate in the international economy. But it may be true that ExxonMobil has felt the burden of sanctions more than the average American business.

When looking at each prong under Penn Central and weighing the factors, a case can be made that a regulatory taking has occurred: ExxonMobil has lost about $1 billion as a result of the Ukraine-Related Sanctions, which were designed to protect global democracy, but have instead proven ineffective and fallen disproportionately on American citizens.

Some may balk at the idea of the federal government compensating corporations for the diminished value of their assets as a result of foreign policy. But under a strict interpretation of the Takings Clause, the concept of temporary partial regulatory takings is still consistent with the underlying constitutional goals. For example, the most common application of the Takings Clause is seen in eminent domain: when the government physically takes your land to build or expand a highway. Your home (private property) is taken for public use (building a highway), and thus you are constitutionally entitled to compensation for the taking. With temporary partial regulatory takings, the idea is the same— the government executes a regulation for some public interest. Here, the economic sanctions against Russia were executed to protect global democracy. The regulation renders corporate assets (private property) effectively valueless. In specific cases, even though the regulatory taking is temporary, the effects of the taking are permanent due to lost opportunity costs. Assuming the claim endures a Penn Central analysis (and that is, admittedly, a big assumption), the injured party, the corporation, is still constitutionally entitled to compensation.

The problem, and why this Comment deems it a "novel" takings claim, is that courts have historically bypassed the Penn Central analysis. Instead, courts that have addressed Fifth Amendment takings challenges under IEEPA either: (1) forego any analysis, but hold that blockings do not, as a matter of law, constitute a taking within the meaning of the Fifth Amendment; or (2) apply a quasi-Agins, due process-type analysis, where sanctions are found to serve an important national security interest but no balancing test is applied. Moreover, to support the rationale that takings claims in the context of IEEPA or foreign policy can never survive, courts have frequently cited or quoted the century-old *Knox v. Lee* case, which poetically states:

> A new tariff, an embargo, a draft, or a war may inevitably bring upon individuals great losses; may, indeed, render valuable property almost valueless. They may destroy the worth of contracts. But whoever supposed that, because of this, a tariff could not be changed, or a non-intercourse act, or an embargo be enacted, or a war be declared? . . . [W]as it ever imagined this was taking private property without compensation or without due process of law?

After all, the rationale makes sense—"governance inherently affects property to some extent and could not function" if every government regulation resulting in the diminution of private property value was grounds for a takings claim.

When the type of takings claim proposed here is taken to its fullest extent, the reality of the federal government paying a mega-corporation $1 billion is bleak—and borderline hysterical. But the theory behind the hyperbolic takings claim is not. Partial regulatory takings claims have been a way to check executive branch power for decades—takings claims force the government to evaluate the purpose and effectiveness of its regulations or pay the price. The thought that goes in to economic sanctions should be no different.

When courts rely on stale sanctions jurisprudence, there is little to no consideration of the long term effects and loss of economic revenue that could marginalize American industries and jobs, as seen historically in the sanctions against China and India. The President's calculation and consideration of economic sanctions should balance the actual threat to the American people and national security against the potential losses to the American economy rather than relying on an overly broad use of power for the sake of implementing questionable foreign policy.

Conclusion

With the growing data on the ineffectiveness of economic sanctions and yet another multinational corporation losing market share to foreign companies, it may be time to reconsider the vast breadth of executive authority in times where there is no danger to the American people, and thus no "public necessity." The proposed novel takings claim introduces a creative and constitutional basis for sharing the costs of public policy through more fair and equitable means.

Economic Sanctions Are Not a Silver Bullet Answer

Peter D. Feaver, Eric B. Lorber

In the following viewpoint, Peter D. Feaver and Eric B. Lorber argue that sanctions alone are not the answer and shouldn't be the first tool used. They claim sanctions work best when partnered with other tools as part of an an integrated, well-considered overall strategy. Feaver is a professor of political science and public policy at Duke University. He is director of the Triangle Institute for Security Studies and director of the Duke Program in American Grand Strategy. Lorber is an attorney in the Washington, DC, office of Gibson, Dunn & Crutcher.

As you read, consider the following questions:

1. What were the unintended consequences of the US imposed sanctions on Russia?
2. How have sanctions evolved over time?
3. Why is it more difficult to narrowly tailor sanctions to achieve specific objectives?

Since 2005, American policy makers have increasingly turned to sophisticated types of economic sanctions as a foreign-policy tool of first resort. From the development of banking sanctions limiting Iran's ability to secure financing from Western capital markets to new sanctions targeting Russia's financial system and the

"The Sanctions Myth", by Peter D. Feaver and Eric B. Lorber, The National Interest, June 15, 2015. Reprinted by permission.

development of its oil resources, US policy makers are touting these innovative tools as extremely powerful while also being tailored and precise. The Obama administration's 2015 National Security Strategy, for example, said that "targeted economic sanctions remain an effective tool for imposing costs on . . . irresponsible actors" and that "our sanctions will continue to be carefully designed and tailored to achieve clear aims while minimizing any unintended consequences for other economic actors, the global economy, and civilian populations."

These sanctions are indeed powerful, and in many respects they represent a marked improvement over earlier generations of economic statecraft. But some of the problems that limited the effectiveness of previous sanctions also limit the effectiveness of these new tools. And the most important lesson from earlier efforts of economic coercion still applies: sanctions work best when they are a tactic incorporated into a well-considered strategy. They falter when they are employed as a substitute for such a strategy.

The new sanctions are better than the old ones in several ways. They are more precise than the "comprehensive" sanctions of the 1990s and are thus more likely to hurt legitimate targets and less likely to hurt innocent bystanders. They are also more effective than the "smart" sanctions (such as travel bans) of the early 2000s, and so less likely to feel like token symbols substituting for real pressure. Their greater effectiveness comes from the way they harness the United States' position as the leader of the global financial system; through a number of mechanisms, the sanctions prevent rogue actors from accessing the US financial system and force legitimate financial institutions to abandon any business with targeted countries and individuals.

But while these sanctions can have significant economic impacts, policy makers overestimate their ability to calibrate and control these tools of economic statecraft. As with earlier forms of economic coercion, it is still difficult to predict their economic or political effects. For example, Barack Obama and his European Union partners clearly intended to ratchet up pressure on Vladimir Putin's Russia only gradually. They resisted more draconian proposals and imposed modest sanctions that, for a long time, seemed to impose little real pain on the targeted sectors—until the sanctions combined with the separate-and-unplanned-for drop in oil prices. Now, the effects of the sanctions in tandem with the oil-price drop have contributed to the near collapse of the ruble and effectively ended foreign direct investment into Russia. This is clearly more than the Obama administration intended or anticipated—though in light of Putin's continued defiance, the White House has referenced this impact as evidence of its tough response.

Likewise, the new sanctions do not avoid one unintended effect that bedeviled earlier forms of economic coercion: the ability of targeted regimes to use the sanctions to amass more political power against their rivals, at least temporarily. In the case of Russia, for example, Putin has used the economic impact of the sanctions to diminish the influence of political and economic elites who oppose many of his policies. The result may be that Russia becomes more authoritarian—and less likely to act in ways that further Western interests.

The developing narrative that increasingly sophisticated sanctions provide policy makers with a silver bullet for addressing intractable national-security issues is wrong. These new sanctions can be powerful, but they often cannot be calibrated to the extent policy makers desire—or to the extent necessary to deliver strategic objectives. Indeed, in many ways their greatest asset is also their most significant liability; because they primarily utilize international financial markets (which is how they are able to create so much leverage), their reach and effects can often be very difficult to predict.

In the middle of the last decade, the United States began employing significantly more sophisticated types of economic sanctions. Using the importance of the dollar in the global financial system, private firms' concern with their business reputations and the fact that the United States is the hub for many key technologies necessary for the development of industries in other countries, the United States found new ways to pressure rogue actors.

In the case of Iran, for example, the United States relied on its position as the financial capital of the world—and one of its largest markets—to force foreign companies to abandon their business with the Islamic Republic. The US Treasury Department threatened those companies with a choice: either they could do business in US financial markets (and have access to US dollars for transactional purposes) or they could do business in Iran, but not both. As a result, a large number of foreign firms shuttered their business operations in Iran, increasing economic pressure on the country. This ability to impose what many countries argued were extraterritorial sanctions helped prevent Iran from easily finding alternative trade and financing partners, and was—at least in part—responsible for bringing the country to the negotiating table to discuss its nuclear program.

Similarly, the United States has imposed sophisticated new sanctions on Russia that move well beyond simple prohibitions on transacting with certain of Vladimir Putin's cronies. These new tools—which target Russia's ability to refinance its massive external debt, as well as prevent the country from developing key energy resources over the medium to long term—leverage advantages enjoyed by the United States: technological superiority and attractive capital markets. A significant component of these sanctions prevents US energy companies from providing cutting-edge technologies to Russian firms that would help those firms develop difficult-to-reach oil resources (such as shale, offshore and Arctic resources). And like the sanctions aimed at isolating Iran from Western financial markets, US and EU sanctions on Russia prohibit Western financial firms from dealing in new debt or equity with more than a thirty-day maturity period, making it exceedingly difficult for Russian companies to secure the necessary financing to service the country's massive debt.

These new forms of economic statecraft have proven powerful. For example, as a partial result of the sanctions, economists are predicting that the Russian economy will shrink by 3.5–4 percent in 2015 and continue contracting in the medium term. Likewise, the Iranian economy is suffering from significant inflation, and according to the Treasury Department, sanctions on the Iranian petroleum industry cost the country $40 billion in revenue in 2014.

Policy makers, seeing the sophisticated nature and powerful impact of these sanctions, have concluded that these new tools of coercion are different from—and a marked improvement on—prior forms of economic punishment. For example, in a December 2014 speech, David S. Cohen, then the under secretary of the treasury for terrorism and financial intelligence, noted that

> we have been able to move away from clunky and heavy-handed instruments of economic power. . . . All of us in this room remember how sanctions used to consist primarily of trade restrictions or wholesale bans on commercial activity. . . . These embargoes rarely created meaningful pressure. Sanctions that focus on bad actors within the financial sector are far more precise and far more effective than traditional trade sanctions.

This perspective is echoed in the 2015 National Security Strategy, which makes clear that these targeted economic sanctions are an effective tool for dealing with threats to the United States and its allies and friends.

As Cohen went on to say in his speech, "Financial power has become an essential component of our country's national-security toolkit. That fact may mean that we are called on to use it more frequently and in more complex ways than we have in previous decades."

But while these sophisticated sanctions have imposed substantial economic costs on Iran and Russia, policy makers' optimism about their usefulness may be excessive. Indeed, it is more difficult than policy makers think to narrowly tailor these tools to achieve particular strategic objectives for at least two reasons.

First, the economic effects of these sanctions are unpredictable. In the case of Russia, the macroeconomic impact of US and EU sanctions—combined with the drop in international oil prices and actions taken by Russian regulators—has undercut the country's economy to a far greater extent than was expected or desired. For example, by March 2015, inflation in Russia had risen to 16.9 percent. This followed on the footsteps of a near run on the country's currency, which was supposedly triggered by the Central Bank of Russia promising to effectively print money to prop up certain companies owned by Putin's confederates and hurt by Western sanctions. By the spring of 2015, Russia had spent approximately $130 billion of its precious currency reserves in an attempt to defend the value of the ruble and prevent it from sliding even further. In addition, by raising interest rates to 17 percent in an attempt to stabilize the ruble, the central bank has likely stymied consumer spending in the near term.

While these economic impacts have been profound, US policy makers did not anticipate them. Nor did they intend to create them. It is fair to say that the collapse of Russia's economy would cause many more problems in the region than it would solve, and if the Obama administration wanted to seriously undermine the Russian economy, it could have easily done so by designating a number of Russian banks and directly freezing them out of the US and European financial sectors. This action would have been a far simpler and more direct way to cause Russia economic pain and bring it to the negotiating table over the Ukraine issue. These new, sophisticated sanctions were instead designed to hurt a specific subset of Russian companies, namely those that are owned or controlled by Putin's inner circle or directly run by the Russian government. Yet, despite the fact that these sanctions are narrowly tailored, they could end up causing economic damage to the Russian economy that would be similar to what would result from a wholesale ban on transacting with certain industries, such as the financial sector.

Second, the political effects of these sophisticated sanctions are also difficult to predict. In the Russian case, US policy makers developed the sanctions in order to target Vladimir Putin's inner circle. If his henchmen were hurt, it was believed, they would pressure the Russian president to adopt a different course in Crimea and eastern Ukraine. And while the sanctions have damaged the economic interests of these individuals, the result has been the opposite of what policy makers intended. Instead of pulling out of Crimea and ceasing Russian support for the rebel forces in Ukraine, Putin requisitioned property of more liberal oligarchs and consolidated the position of hard-liners within the political, military and economic sectors. For example, in late 2014, Russian authorities seized Russian businessman Vladimir Yevtushenkov's oil company, Bashneft, and effectively nationalized the company in what was seen as an attempt to secure resources for the Russian government and to reallocate the company to Putin's allies.

Likewise, Putin has reportedly sidelined even those conservative oligarchs who have supported him thus far during the crisis in favor of relying on the advice of a small group of military and security officials. These officials have further encouraged Russian support of separatists in eastern Ukraine and a generally confrontational approach to the United States and the European Union. In effect, the sanctions may have made it more difficult for the United States to achieve its goals in the conflict; by isolating Putin and damaging the Russian economy, the sanctions have caused Putin to consolidate his power and limit his inner circle to those advisers who advocate policies at odds with US interests.

While the use of economic statecraft has become more sophisticated in the last decade, tailoring these tools to achieve the desired political effects remains exceedingly difficult, and US policy makers should not be lulled into believing that these new forms of coercion can be perfectly calibrated to address every foreign-policy challenge. And though they may be more effective than the "comprehensive" sanctions of the 1990s or the "smart" sanctions of the early 2000s, these new levers present a new set of complications for policy makers, such as being significantly more powerful and difficult to control than anticipated.

To overcome these obstacles and ensure that these new sanctions are more likely to achieve US strategic objectives, the

Obama administration can take a number of steps. First, it should be wary of relying on these new sanctions as tools of first resort. These levers are attractive in large part because they can be imposed unilaterally (or with minimal allied support) and quickly, and are seemingly risk-free in comparison to other forms of coercion such as using military force. In the case of Russia, for instance, the administration was quick to target Vladimir Putin's clique using sanctions because many of the alternatives were unpalatable. Yet this rush to react also created a number of unanticipated consequences, such as Western businesses that had assets with Russian companies that were indirectly and opaquely owned by some of Putin's collaborators finding their economic interests unexpectedly harmed. Likewise, as the recent debates in Congress over the Iranian nuclear deal have shown, unwinding sanctions can often be more difficult than imposing them, and turning to sanctions as a knee-jerk reaction can often cause significant complications down the road. To be sure, economic sanctions may still often end up being the best alternative to doing nothing or to escalating to military force, but policy makers need to realize that many of the arguments against those other two options may also apply in some measure against sanctions.

Second, and relatedly, US policy makers should study the likely impacts of these sophisticated sanctions more carefully prior to imposing them. In targeting a number of Russia's financial institutions, for example, the administration believed that it had found a way to threaten Russian companies' ability to service their massive debt, as well as the health of the Russian economy in the medium and long term. While such damage seems probable, US policy makers did not anticipate that the sanctions would nearly cause the Russian currency to collapse or lead Vladimir Putin to consolidate his authoritarian rule, making the achievement of US objectives more difficult. The Obama administration would be well served to create an interagency working group that closely examines the likely economic and political impact of these new sanctions before imposing them. Yet we must not kid ourselves about our ability to predict effects with great confidence. These sanctions are more powerful than earlier generations of "smart" sanctions precisely because they have a multiplier effect beyond the direct control, and thus beyond the confident predictions, of policy makers.

Third, and most importantly, policy makers should not rely on these tools in place of a strategy, but rather should incorporate them into a broader strategy for safeguarding US interests. In the case of Russia, for example, the Obama administration has seemingly relied on sanctions to impose economic pain on the country in the hopes of convincing it to pull out of Crimea and to cease its support of rebels in eastern Ukraine. But sanctions—even sophisticated ones—are rarely effective alone, and must be used in conjunction with other tools of diplomacy to have much chance of success. Rather than imposing sanctions on target countries and rogue actors and hoping that they can cause enough pain, policy makers should carefully consider how to use sanctions, threats of force, negotiations and other forms of diplomacy in a coordinated way to achieve US objectives.

In the end, sanctions will contribute the most in those cases when any tool of statecraft will be most effective: when the leaders know where they want to go, have a good idea of how to get there and are committed to expending the resources—financial, military, moral and political—to get there. Sanctions will not be sufficient substitutes if the leaders lack such strategic insight and resolve.

Periodical and Internet Sources Bibliography

The following articles have been selected to supplement the diverse views presented in this chapter.

Efraim Chalamish, "Economic Sanctions Popular But Not Painless," *Global Finance*, October 2017. https://www.gfmag.com /magazine/october-2017/economic-sanctions-popular-not -painless.

Daniel W. Drezner, "Let the Debate About Economic Sanctions Begin," *Washington Post*, March 30, 2016. https://www .washingtonpost.com/posteverything/wp/2016/03/30/let -the-debate-about-economic-sanctions-begin/?utm_term= .f9a678e11536.

Economist, "Sudan's Economy Is in Trouble, Even Without Sanctions," October 14, 2017. https://www.economist.com/news/middle -east-and-africa/21730152-america-has-lifted-trade-embargo -rapid-growth-will-not-be-easy.

Pia Figuerola, "Economic Sanctions' Effectiveness in a World with Interdependent Networks and Powerful MNCs: The Role of Governance in the Target State," University of Pennsylvania, January 1, 2015. https://repository.upenn.edu/curej/190.

Front News International, "New Economic Sanctions Against Russia May Have More Tangible Impact," August 7, 2017. https:// frontnews.eu/news/en/9917/New-economic-sanctions-against -Russia-may-have-more-tangible-impact.

Richard N. Haass, "Economic Sanctions: Too Much of a Bad Thing," Brooking's Policy Briefs, June 1, 1998. https://www.brookings .edu/research/economic-sanctions-too-much-of-a-bad-thing.

Shellie Karabell, "Why Russian Sanctions Haven't Worked," *Forbes*, August 14, 2017. https://www.forbes.com/sites /shelliekarabell/2017/08/14/why-russian-sanctions-havent -worked/#5e8e8e7234d8.

Alvaro Morales Salto-Weis, "Economic Sanctions After Brexit: What Roles Should the Public and Private Sector Play?" Atlantic Council, October 3, 2017. http://www.atlanticcouncil.org/events /past-events/economic-sanctions-after-brexit-what-roles-should -the-public-and-private-sector-play.

Richard Nephew, "The Future of Economic Sanctions in a Global Economy," Center on Global Energy Policy, May 21, 2015. http:// energypolicy.columbia.edu/research/report/future-economic -sanctions-global-economy.

Public Radio International, "Sudanese Look Forward to a Brighter Future, with US Sanctions Ending Oct. 12," October 7, 2017. https://www.pri.org/stories/2017-10-07/sudanese-look-forward -brighter-future-us-sanctions-ending-oct-12.

Samuel Rubenfeld, "Trump Will Continue Using Behavioral Sanctions, Unlikely to Change Cuba Much," *Wall Street Journal*, January 6, 2017. https://blogs.wsj.com /riskandcompliance/2017/01/06/trump-will-continue-using -behavioral-sanctions-unlikely-to-change-cuba-much.

For Further Discussion

Chapter 1

1. How does Drezner's evaluation of the Iraq smart sanctions compare to Meyssan's evaluation?
2. Devarajan and Mottaghi cite examples of how lifting economic sanctions can be beneficial to the world market, but in what ways might lifted sanctions hurt or hinder the world market?

Chapter 2

1. Is the threat of sanctions as effective as imposing sanctions? If so, why?
2. Despite their track record, why do policymakers continue to employ economic sanctions?

Chapter 3

1. How can policymakers distinguish between a sponsor and host of terrorism?
2. In what ways can a state sponsor of terrorism affect their status?

Chapter 4

1. Considering both Early and Warren's advice, when should economic sanctions be employed?
2. How might the public perception of sanctions alter their use in the future?

Organizations to Contact

The editors have compiled the following list of organizations concerned with the issues debated in this book. The descriptions are derived from materials provided by the organizations. All have publications or information available for interested readers. The list was compiled on the date of publication of the present volume; the information provided here may change. Be aware that many organizations take several weeks or longer to respond to inquiries, so allow as much time as possible.

Amnesty International
1 Easton Street
London, WC1X 0DW, UK
+44-20-74135500
email: contactus@amnesty.org
website: www.amnesty.org/en/

Amnesty International is a global movement of more than seven million people who take injustice personally. We are campaigning for a world where human rights are enjoyed by all.

The Brooking Institute
1775 Massachusetts Ave., NW
Washington, DC 20036
(202) 797.6000
email: communications@brookings.edu
website: www.brookings.edu/

The Brookings Institution is a nonprofit public policy organization based in Washington, DC. Our mission is to conduct in-depth research that leads to new ideas for solving problems facing society at the local, national and global level.

The Carnegie Endowment for International Peace
1779 Massachusetts Avenue NW
Washington, DC 20036-2103
(202) 483 7600
website: http://carnegieendowment.org/

The Carnegie Endowment for International Peace is a unique global network of policy research centers in Russia, China, Europe, the Middle East, India, and the United States. Our mission, dating back more than a century, is to advance peace through analysis and development of fresh policy ideas and direct engagement and collaboration with decision makers in government, business, and civil society.

Center For International Policy
2000 M Street NW, Suite 720
Washington, DC 20036
(202) 232-3317
email: cip@ciponline.org
website: www.ciponline.org/

The Center for International Policy promotes cooperation, transparency and accountability in global relations. Through research and advocacy, our programs address the most urgent threats to our planet: war, corruption, inequality and climate change.

The Center for Strategic and International Studies
1616 Rhode Island Avenue, NW
Washington, DC 20036
(202) 887-0200
email: webmaster@csis.org
website: www.csis.org/

The Center for Strategic and International Studies (CSIS) is a bipartisan, nonprofit policy research organization dedicated to providing strategic insights and policy solutions to help decision makers chart a course toward a better world.

Council on Foreign Relations
58 East 68th Street
New York, NY 10065
(212) 434-9400
email: communications@cfr.org
website: www.cfr.org/

The Council on Foreign Relations (CFR) is an independent, nonpartisan membership organization, think tank, and publisher dedicated to being a resource for its members, government officials, business executives, journalists, educators and students, civic and religious leaders, and other interested citizens in order to help them better understand the world and the foreign policy choices facing the United States and other countries.

Global Affairs Canada
125 Sussex Drive
Ottawa, Ontario, Canada
K1A 0G2
(800) 267-8376
website: www.international.gc.ca/

Global Affairs Canada manages Canada's diplomatic and consular relations, promotes the country's international trade and leads Canada's international development and humanitarian assistance.

Global Policy Forum
866 UN Plaza, Suite 4050
New York, NY 10017
(646) 553-3460
email: gpf@globalpolicy.org
website: www.globalpolicy.org

Global Policy Forum is an independent policy watchdog that monitors the work of the United Nations and scrutinizes global policymaking. We promote accountability and citizen participation in decisions on peace and security, social justice and international law.

The Handa Centre for the Study of Terrorism and Political Violence
School of International Relations
University of St. Andrews
Arts Faculty Building, Library Park, The Scores
St Andrews, Fife, KY16 9AX
Scotland, UK
+44 (0) 1334 462935
email: gm39@st-andrews.ac.uk
website: www.st-andrews.ac.uk/~cstpv/

The Handa Centre for the Study of Terrorism and Political Violence (CSTPV) is dedicated to the study of the causes, dynamics, characteristics and consequences of terrorism and related forms of political violence. In doing so, it is committed to rigorous, evidence-based, scholarly analysis that is policy-relevant but independent.

Office of Foreign Assets Control
US Department of the Treasury, Treasury Annex,
1500 Pennsylvania Avenue, NW
Washington, DC 20220
(800) 540-6322
email: ofac_feedback@treasury.gov

The Office of Foreign Assets Control (OFAC) of the US Department of the Treasury administers and enforces economic and trade sanctions based on US foreign policy and national security goals against targeted foreign countries and regimes, terrorists, international narcotics traffickers, those engaged in activities related to the proliferation of weapons of mass destruction, and other threats to the national security, foreign policy or economy of the United States.

The Peterson Institute for International Economics
1750 Massachusetts Avenue, NW
Washington, DC 20036-1903
(202) 328-9000
email: comments@piie.com
website: https://piie.com/

The Peterson Institute for International Economics (PIIE) is a private, nonpartisan nonprofit institution whose purpose is to identify and analyze important issues to make globalization beneficial and sustainable for the people of the United States and the world and then develop and communicate practical new approaches for dealing with those issues.

United Nations Security Council
405 East 42nd Street
New York, NY, 10017
(212) 963-7160
email: contactnewscentre@un.org
Website: www.un.org/en/sc/

The UN Charter established six main organs of the United Nations, including the Security Council. It gives primary responsibility for maintaining international peace and security to the Security Council, which may meet whenever peace is threatened.

Bibliography of Books

Robert D. Blackwill and Jennifer M. Harris. *War by Other Means: Geoeconomics and Statecraft*. Cambridge, MA: Harvard University Press, 2017.

Eliot Cohen. *The Big Stick: The Limits of Soft Power and the Necessity of Military Force*. New York, NY: Basic Books, 2017.

Bryan R. Early. *Busted Sanctions: Explaining Why Economic Sanctions Fail*. Palo Alto, CA: Stanford University Press, 2015.

William Easterly. *The Tyranny of Experts: Economists, Dictators, and the Forgotten Rights of the Poor*. New York, NY: Basic Books, 2014.

Joy Gordon. *Invisible War: The United States and the Iraq Sanctions*. Cambridge, MA: Harvard University Press, 2012.

Richard Haass. *A World in Disarray: American Foreign Policy and the Crisis of the Old Order*. New York, NY: Penguin, 2018.

Stephan Haggard and Marcus Noland. *Hard Target: Sanctions, Inducements, and the Case of North Korea*. Palo Alto, CA: Stanford University Press, 2017.

Craig Hayden. *The Rhetoric of Soft Power: Public Diplomacy in Global Contexts*. Lanham, MD: Lexington Books, 2012.

Michael V. Hayden. *Playing to the Edge: American Intelligence in the Age of Terror*. New York, NY: Penguin, 2017.

Eric Hershberg and William M. LeoGrande. *A New Chapter in US-Cuba Relations: Social, Political, and Economic Implications*. New York, NY: Springer, 2016.

Richard Nephew. *The Art of Sanctions: A View from the Field*. New York, NY: Columbia University Press, 2017.

Steve Smith, Tim Dunne and Amelia Hadfield. *Foreign Policy: Theories, Actors, Cases*. Oxford, United Kingdom: Oxford University Press, 2016.

Etel Solingen. *Sanctions, Statecraft, and Nuclear Proliferation*. Cambridge, United Kingdom: Cambridge University Press, 2012.

Index